6749

The Right to Die

THE RIGHT TO DIE

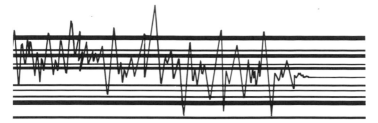

Public Controversy, Private Matter

Kathlyn Gay

The Millbrook Press
Brookfield, Connecticut

Issue and Debate

Photos courtesy of AP/Wide World Photos: pp. 12, 15, 21, 28, 33, 38, 46, 57, 78, 85, 93; Bettmann Archive: p. 25; Rothco: p. 49; Photo Researchers: pp. 59 (© Blair Seitz), 100 (© Esther Shapiro); UPI/Bettmann: pp. 72, 91; Choice in Dying, Inc.: pp. 86, 107; Clement Allard/CanaPress: p. 103.

Library of Congress Cataloging-in-Publication Data
Gay, Kathlyn.
The right to die : public controversy, private matter / by Kathlyn Gay.
p.   cm.—(Issue and debate)
Includes bibliographical references and index.
ISBN 1-56294-325-1 (lib. bdg.)
1. Right to die—Moral and ethical aspects.   2. Euthanasia—Moral and ethical aspects.   3. Assisted suicide—Moral and ethical aspects.   4. Death—Social aspects.   I. Title.   II. Series.
R726.G39   1993
179'.7—dc20   92-32201   CIP

Published by The Millbrook Press
2 Old New Milford Road
Brookfield, Connecticut 06804

Contents

The Right
to Die

Is There a Right to Die?

At first glance, the question of whether a person has a right to die appears to have a simple answer: Everyone comes to the end of life in due time and dying is inevitable. So of course there is a right to die, many people say.

Yet no such right, in contrast to the right of free speech or the right of citizens to vote, is spelled out in the U.S. Constitution. Nevertheless, our society accepts the common-law right of self-determination and bodily integrity, which means that unless you are a minor or incompetent, you have the right to make informed choices about your medical care, and you can refuse certain procedures such as blood transfusions. It also means surgeons cannot legally perform an operation without a patient's consent, unless there is an emergency. But the question of whether there is a right to die may arise when a terminally ill person requests aid in dying or refuses medical treatment to hasten the dying process.

Only a few decades ago, terminally ill people had few choices to make about their care. Doctors and other health care professionals did not have the heroic or extraordinary means, as certain medical procedures are called today, to keep a person alive. Neither could they bring people back to life after breathing or circulation stopped. Few "miracle" drugs and little lifesaving equipment were available.

Today, scientific advances and medical technology in most industrialized countries have helped people live longer. They also have prolonged dying. As a result, some very ill people may linger for months or years in pain or in a coma (a form of unconsciousness). Prolonged dying can be agonizing not only for the patient but also for family and friends. Consider the tragic circumstances surrounding Karen Ann Quinlan of New Jersey and Nancy Cruzan of Missouri. They were both kept alive by artificial means, prompting much debate about the right to die.

Karen Ann Quinlan. In 1975, twenty-one-year-old Karen Ann Quinlan was at a party, celebrating a birthday. She had eaten little for two or three days prior to the party, and also had taken some drugs—perhaps tranquilizers, but no one is sure. At the celebration, Quinlan consumed a few alcoholic drinks and suddenly began to act strangely. Her friends took her to their home, but later when they checked on her, they found she was not breathing and called for a rescue squad to rush her to the hospital.

Quinlan's breathing was restored, and in the hospital she was connected to a respirator, a machine to help her breathe. But the lack of oxygen during the time when her breathing was interrupted caused permanent brain damage. She was in a coma from which she would not recover, but she was not considered brain-dead.

To determine brain death, physicians usually follow Harvard Medical School guidelines. One criterion is that the person demonstrates no response to stimuli; another is that the person's electroencephalogram (EEG) is flat. The EEG is a graph that shows whether the brain emits waves of electricity. A flat line on the graph in most cases indicates that there is no electrical activity and that all brain functions have ceased.

According to medical reports, tests showed that Quinlan had brain-wave activity, and she responded to stimuli. A neurologist (an expert on the nervous system) concluded that Quinlan did not meet the Harvard criteria for brain death and ordered continued use of a respirator. Liquid nourishment was administered through a feeding tube.

Quinlan's parents were convinced their daughter would not want to be kept alive by artificial means. After conferring with their priest, they asked the doctor to disconnect their daughter's respirator. But the doctor refused on the grounds that he would be committing murder.

The parents believed they should have been able to act on their daughter's behalf and sued the hospital. But a superior court judge ruled that the state, through the hospital, had a duty to continue life support for Quinlan; her parents could not determine her fate.

In a 1976 appeal to the New Jersey Supreme Court, the lower court ruling was overturned. The higher court said that Quinlan's right to privacy—the right to make her own decisions—had been infringed and that her parents could assert this right for her. As a result, she was removed from the respirator and taken to a nursing home.

Many people thought Quinlan would die without a machine to help her breathe, but instead her body continued to live. She was kept alive with nourishment delivered through the feeding tube. Her parents believed that food and water should be provided, even though some people argued then, and argue still, that forced feedings are just another artificial means of maintaining a life that is more like that of a vegetable than of a person.

Joseph and Julia Quinlan pose with a photograph of their daughter Karen Ann on her twenty-fifth birthday. Karen Ann had been in a coma for four years by this time and remained in a persistent vegetative state until her death five years later.

Karen was in a persistent vegetative state (PVS), or permanent coma. In such a state, the brain stem, which controls reflex actions, functions; but the cerebral cortex, or thinking and memory part of the brain, does not. Quinlan remained in a nursing home for ten years after her respirator was disconnected, and in 1985 her body died. [1]

Nancy Cruzan. The Cruzan family in Missouri faced a situation similar to that of the Quinlans. In 1983, Nancy Cruzan, who was twenty-five years old at the time, was driving on an icy road when her car slid and crashed, throwing her from the vehicle. She landed unconscious, face down in a ditch, where she nearly suffocated. Although paramedics started her breathing again, she was without sufficient oxygen for at least thirteen minutes. This resulted in brain damage that left her in a permanent coma. Her muscles moved involuntarily, her eyes opened and closed, but she was unconscious and unable to think or communicate.

When doctors determined that Nancy Cruzan was in a vegetative state, her parents, Joe and Joyce Cruzan, like the Quinlans, said they knew their daughter would not want to be kept alive with machines. They requested that hospital officials disconnect all life supports, including feeding tubes inserted into Nancy's stomach. But medical personnel refused to withdraw food and water, arguing that if these were not provided as basic care, they would be "killing" Nancy by starvation and dehydration. The hospital did not consider nourishment and fluids to be artificial life support.

In 1988, the Cruzans sought help from the courts to try to carry out their daughter's wishes. A county court judge ruled that the feeding tube could be removed. In the judge's opinion, Nancy Cruzan had not received equal protection under the law when the hospital refused to comply with her wishes as stated by her parents.

However, the state immediately appealed the decision to the Missouri Supreme Court, which overturned the lower court ruling in a 5–4 decision. The higher court concluded that the state could abide only by the patient's *declared* wishes, not those as stated by surrogates, or substitutes. Under Missouri law, Joe and Joyce Cruzan did not have the authority to act for their daughter. Since the state had a responsibility to protect life, food and water were required as basic care.

Over the next few years, Joe and Joyce Cruzan, who visited their daughter daily, agonized over their inability to help her achieve a peaceful ending. They, along with their two other daughters, believed Nancy had died in the car accident, and the feeding tubes were only keeping her body alive.

In one of his first public interviews, Joe Cruzan said he could not agree with the argument that the removal of hydration and nutrition would be the actual cause of Nancy's death. Rather, he said, "It's the treatment that's withdrawn. It's the technology that's pulled away. If you take away the artificial procedure . . . she will die because she doesn't have the capability to swallow."

Joyce Cruzan pointed out wearily, "When they [doctors] talk about removing a respirator, they don't say anything about suffocating people. But when they talk about removing nutrition and hydration, it's always starvation, starvation."[2]

The Cruzan case eventually reached the U.S. Supreme Court (*Cruzan v. Director, Missouri Department of Health*). In 1990, the justices ruled that a person has the constitutional right to refuse life-support treatment, including food and water. It was a historic decision, the first high court ruling on this issue, which, in effect, said a

Nancy Cruzan was a vital twenty-five-year-old before a car accident left her in a permanent coma. Sustained by life-support treatment, she was described as "an unconscious shell in a room full of strangers."

person has the right to die without interference. But the justices also declared that any state could limit that right for incompetent persons—those unable to express their wishes.

Chief Justice William Rehnquist, who delivered the majority opinion, explained that "not all incompetent patients will have loved ones available to serve as surrogate decision-makers." Even if family members or guardians are available, they may not act to protect patients. Thus, the Court ruled that Missouri had the right to adopt a standard requiring "clear and convincing" proof that a guardian was expressing "a patient's desire to have hydration and nutrition withdrawn."[3]

Once more the Cruzans were barred from carrying out what they believed were their daughter's wishes. But not long after the U.S. Supreme Court ruling, the Cruzans were granted a second hearing before the county court judge who had ruled originally on their case. The Cruzans had new evidence to present. Several of Nancy's former coworkers testified for the first time about long conversations they had had with Nancy, who clearly stated that she would not want to be kept alive by artificial means. Two coworkers said they had not come forward years before because they had not known about the case.

Because of the testimony, the county judge ruled that Nancy Cruzan's wishes were clear and convincing, as required by the Supreme Court. The Cruzans were finally able to carry out those wishes on December 14, 1990, and the feeding tube was removed. Protest groups tried last-minute legal maneuvers to prevent the removal of the feeding tube. When those failed, they invaded the hospital to try to reconnect the apparatus and even threatened to take Nancy away. But the comatose woman was allowed to exist without life support. Her family maintained their vigil until Nancy died on December 26, 1990. In her father's words, Nancy was "free at last . . . thank God."[4]

Euthanasia. The Quinlan and Cruzan cases not only sparked questions about a person's right to die, but also focused attention on "mercy killing," or euthanasia. The term euthanasia is actually an English-language version of a Greek phrase *eu thanatos*, meaning "well death," or dying without pain. Dictionaries define euthanasia as "an act or method of causing death painlessly" or "the practice of killing individuals who are hopelessly sick or injured for reasons of mercy." The term implies deliberately ending a life or hastening the onset of death. Usually, people equate euthanasia with the idea of preventing further suffering for terminally ill people.

However, medical personnel, theologians, bioethicists (people who study the ethics or morality of medical actions), and many nonprofessionals make a distinction between passive euthanasia and active euthanasia. In general, passive euthanasia is allowing a person to die by withholding or withdrawing treatment. Respirators, heart and lung machines, feeding tubes, and other mechanical means of maintaining life are not used when there is no known chance that a patient will be cured. The idea is to stop treatment and shorten the dying process, preventing a prolonged death.

"To stop treatment is really a decision to stop doing what is no longer of real benefit to the patient and what has become unreasonably burdensome . . . to step aside and allow the dying to happen," noted a spokesperson for the Park Ridge Center for the Study of Health, Faith, and Ethics, a Chicago "think tank" of diverse religious, health care, and academic leaders. According to the group, most people today believe that passive euthanasia is morally acceptable because it allows a terminally ill person to die "naturally."⁵

Active euthanasia, on the other hand, is a much more complex and controversial matter. Active euthanasia is defined as actually killing someone in an act of kindness, such as injecting a lethal drug to help a person end his or her life.

Some people consider assisted suicide—providing the means for a person to commit suicide—as a form of active euthanasia. Others, however, make a distinction between assisted suicide and actions that directly bring about a person's death.

Assisted suicide includes the type of action taken by Timothy Quill, a New York physician who helped a leukemia patient end her life. In an article published in the March 7, 1991, issue of the *New England Journal of Medicine*, Quill explained that his patient, whom he called Diane, had been consulting him for eight years. He had informed Diane about the types of cancer treatment available, such as chemotherapy and bone marrow transplants, and their chances for success. But she refused these courses of treatment because of the adverse side effects and asked for help to die peacefully at home. Quill suggested that Diane contact the Hemlock Society, a national organization that promotes rational suicide, or "self-deliverance" from a terminal illness.

Diane later called Quill to ask for a prescription for barbiturates (sleeping pills), one of the drugs the Hemlock Society recommends for terminally ill patients who want to commit suicide. Quill carefully considered the morality of such an action and decided that he was justified in honoring her request. He provided her with a prescription for barbiturates, explaining how many pills would be lethal. As Diane's disease progressed and her discomfort increased, Quill, along with Diane's family and friends, made every attempt to comfort and care for her. But one day Diane decided she did not want to suffer any longer. She took an overdose of sleeping pills and died.[6]

Whether or not active euthanasia and assisted suicide should be permitted in our society is at the crux of the right-to-die debate. In the debate, one group may take a stand in favor of euthanasia and the right to die. Another group may be totally opposed to euthanasia and claim a right to life. But for many individuals, questions surrounding euthanasia are not easily resolved. Exploring the issues requires consideration of varied ethical, medical, and legal factors as well as consideration of diverse beliefs, values, and traditions in the United States.

Why the Public Debate? Frequently people argue the pros and cons of euthanasia because of their concern about the manner in which they will die. "As fast as we have been trying to figure out how to allow people to die more peacefully, we keep improving the technology that makes it all the harder to do," according to Daniel Callahan, director of the well-known Hastings Center, a medical ethics research institute based in Briarcliff Manor, New York.[7]

A related concern is the fear expressed by many people that medical practitioners will not be able to provide the means to control their pain should they become seriously ill. Better treatment for terminally ill patients in extreme pain would curb the current demand for active euthanasia, many medical experts say.

Yet pain is not the only fear. Many people also are afraid that a disease could destroy or seriously diminish their mental and physical abilities. As people live longer, they worry that they may become dependent and have to call on younger family members to help with basic care, such as bathing and feeding. Or they dread ending their days in a nursing home. In the opinion of Betsy Davenport, a Portland, Oregon, psychologist, some people feel that it is "preferable to die than to be dependent." Davenport believes that a certain percentage of those who favor active euthanasia have such a strong need for independence that "they will not depend on anyone else for custodial care because to them it is 'undignified' to be bathed 'like a baby' . . . dignity is more valuable than life itself."[8]

Economic factors also play a part in the widespread interest in euthanasia. The high costs of long-term medical care prompt people to consider the burden of extending their lives and prolonging the dying process. High medical costs may also have a subtle or direct influence on whether family members encourage euthanasia for dependent elders or severely disabled relatives.

Finally, another contributing factor in the euthanasia debate is our society's emphasis on individual liberty and the freedom to make choices. People generally want autonomy—to make their own decisions about highly personal matters that range from childbearing to religious beliefs to managing their own dying.

However, society places limits on civil liberties, because individual acts frequently have an effect on other people and sometimes on society as a whole. Certainly an act of euthanasia can have an impact on family and friends as well as others in a community. Health care workers, for example, have much at stake in the question of whether to accommodate a person's request for euthanasia. Consider the case of Donald Cowart, a former Air Force pilot, who endured months of excruciating suffering during medical treatments for severe burns.

In 1973, at the age of twenty-six, Cowart was burned over more than 65 percent of his body when leaking gas in a field exploded, killing his father and sending him running, in flames, for half a mile. When a farmer found him,

In 1983, ten years after being badly burned in a gas explosion, Dax Cowart (right) appeared with University of Texas Law School professor John Robertson at a seminar for doctors. Although he survived the accident, Cowart believes his rights were violated when he received life-sustaining treatment against his wishes.

Cowart asked for a gun to kill himself, but the farmer refused and called an ambulance. Cowart also requested that he not be taken to the hospital and that emergency personnel let him die. But health care professionals were duty-bound to administer lifesaving measures and, when his condition stabilized, to treat him.

That treatment included daily baths in a chlorine bleach solution to clean his raw sores. He also was subjected to numerous operations for skin grafts and amputations. He lost both his eyes and nearly all his fingers, and he had to learn to walk again. After he was released from the hospital, Cowart tried to commit suicide several times and insisted that he should have been allowed to die.

Cowart eventually decided to continue his education and completed law school, changing his name to Dax to reflect what he called his more "cerebral" self. As Dax Cowart he has spoken frequently at conferences on medical ethics.[9]

In spite of Cowart's apparent success in achieving a positive role in life, he maintains to this day that hospital staff consistently violated his right to self-determination. He believes individuals have the moral right to make decisions about life-sustaining measures. Yet medical personnel felt they had a moral obligation to provide lifesaving treatment for Cowart and had a right to act according to their professional ethics and values. The conflict raised ethical and legal questions that are discussed today as part of the euthanasia and right-to-die debate.

One of the major questions is: Who decides? Should medical personnel who may be opposed to euthanasia on moral, legal, and professional grounds help a patient carry out his or her wish to die? Should legislatures make decisions about death and dying? Religious leaders? Ethicists? Families? Should there be limits to a person's right to die? If so, how should they be enforced?

Many euthanasia questions, like these, do not have absolute right or wrong answers. To complicate matters even further, euthanasia questions are tied in with other social issues, such as how to meet the needs of families who must deal with the heavy financial burden of health care for profoundly handicapped and incompetent members, or how to change society's negative attitudes toward disabled individuals. Because of space limitations, these and other related issues can only be touched upon briefly in this book.

The cases and stories presented on these pages are not meant to show what should or should not be done in response to every right-to-die or euthanasia issue. Rather they represent actions that individuals have taken and the continuing struggle within society to deal with these complex issues.

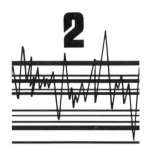

Past and Present
Views on Euthanasia

When the ancient Greeks used the phrase *eu thanatos*, they were talking about not only dying well but also bringing about death—their own or someone else's—in a reasonable and composed manner. Killing oneself or helping another die could only be done for acceptable reasons. A person who wished to die had to be seriously ill with a painful disease, overcome with grief, or in disgrace. Suicide and euthanasia were thought to be ignoble if committed for cowardly rather than dignified reasons, as determined by cultural beliefs and attitudes.

Some committed suicide by drinking hemlock, a drink distilled from a poisonous plant. This was the drink that killed Socrates, the famed Greek teacher and philosopher. Socrates spent his days teaching young people how to think logically and develop reasonable codes of conduct, ideas that challenged accepted teachings. As a result, authorities saw him as a person who corrupted youth, and eventually they arrested him.

Although Socrates could have stopped teaching and had the opportunity to escape into exile, he chose to be tried by a jury. He could not denounce what he saw as the truth. When the jury condemned him to death, he ac-

Condemned to death for corrupting the
young, and refusing to escape into
exile, Socrates toasted the gods and
drank a cup of hemlock poison.

cepted the penalty and carried it out himself, because he also believed it was a noble act to obey the laws of the state.

The idea of a noble death carried over to early Roman society. A person who no longer felt useful or suffered disgrace might find suicide the acceptable way to die.

Not all Greeks or Romans thought euthanasia was morally acceptable, however. Those who opposed the idea argued that the gods expected people to live out their lives no matter what the circumstances. According to such a view, pain was a form of punishment for past misdeeds.

Other Views from the Past. Early Judaic and Christian beliefs greatly altered ideas about managing one's own death and dying with dignity. Judeo-Christian doctrine held—and still holds—that God ordained life and that each life is sacred. As Christianity spread during the second and third centuries, church doctrine declared that an individual's life and death were dependent on God's will. Later, Christians accepted the dogma that mortals should endure whatever hardships might befall them, because this helped to assure immortality (eternal life after death). Christian creed absolutely forbade taking a life.

Such a view was reinforced in the writings of Thomas Aquinas, a Catholic theologian who believed that any type of euthanasia was against the commandment "Thou shalt not kill." Aquinas considered suicide especially harmful, because dying by one's own hand did not allow a person enough time to repent of her or his sins. Eventually, religious and legal codes in Europe declared that suicide was self-murder, and attempted suicide became a criminal act.

From about the fourteenth century on, Europeans became more educated and interested in science, and people's attitudes about euthanasia began to change. Some rejected the belief that illness, pain, and other misery were punishment for sin. Philosophers and physicians began to write about and discuss humane or less painful ways of dying.

At the same time, new medical and scientific knowledge made it possible to extend life. As a result, some people argued against medical intervention that lengthened the dying process and called for the use of drugs such as morphine to ease suffering and even to bring about a merciful death. A few even argued that active euthanasia should be a legal option available for patients with painful and incurable ailments. [1]

During the late 1800s and early 1900s, some medical and legal scholars in Europe and the United States actively promoted the idea of mercy killing and people's right to decide for themselves when they would die. Doctors became increasingly concerned about their responsibility to act on behalf of dying patients who were tortured by pain.

Some court cases also focused on euthanasia. Several revolved around parents who felt they were acting mercifully when they killed their incurably brain-damaged or physically impaired children. Although the parents were charged with murder or manslaughter (a lesser crime), juries either acquitted them or judges released them on probation, apparently convinced that the parents could not cope with a handicapped child or that mercy killing was appropriate in these cases. [2]

Hitler's Corrupt Ideas. Views on euthanasia changed again after many Americans and Europeans learned about the despicable acts of the Nazis under German dictator Adolf Hitler. During World War II, the Nazis launched a secret euthanasia program that they claimed was mercy killing but was actually a calculated and cruel extermination of people the Nazis labeled "useless eaters." Millions of Jews, Gypsies, homosexuals, and others considered

After World War II, inspections of the
remains of Nazi concentration camps
revealed the evil of Hitler's "mercy
killing" programs. Crematoriums like this
one were used to dispose of the bodies.

"valueless" were murdered. Among them were about 100,000 mentally and physically disabled people who were taken from institutions and transported to isolated buildings where they were gassed.

Hitler engineered the mass killings, now known as the Holocaust, to rid his society of what he called "lesser" beings and to create a "racially pure" Germany. Many accounts of the Nazi atrocities have emerged over the years. And today some Americans and Europeans wonder and worry about euthanasia policies that could lead to a situation like that of Nazi Germany. Opponents of euthanasia fear that if mercy killing is allowed, eventually governments may set up programs to do away with unwanted members of society.

However, Hitler and the Nazis used the term euthanasia in a deceptive way to cover up their program of mass murder. The Nazis were able to carry out their evil deeds because they had complete control of the society. In democratic societies, euthanasia would be based on humane principles, advocates contend. Euthanasia would be allowed only to prevent suffering and to assist in a dignified death. Proponents say that any laws or policies making euthanasia legal would have to include protection of the incompetent and powerless.

Quality of Life. Today, those who favor the idea of managing one's death believe that quality of life may determine whether a person chooses to die. People weigh the quality of life in a variety of ways. For example, a person may decide after repeated surgeries and chemotherapy for cancer that quality of life means living the rest of one's days without further invasive medical treatments, even if that hurries death. Or a patient might hasten death if qualities of life such as being able to interact with others or being able to live with dignity are gone.

Advocates of the right to die also believe human life cannot be equated with a mere biological existence. Simply being alive is not the same as "having a life." Some people believe that life ends when an individual is no longer able to function as a person.

The question of what constitutes being a person—or personhood—not only is part of right-to-die issues but also is closely aligned with the abortion debate. In fact, abortion and euthanasia issues often prompt similar arguments. For example, some people contend that life begins at conception, and a fetus (a growing embryo in the womb) is a person; therefore abortion is the same as murder. Others argue that a person does not exist until birth or until the brain functions of the fetus have developed sufficiently to allow independent life. Using this reasoning, someone who is already born but has lost higher brain functions is no longer a person.

The question of personhood will not be resolved quickly, if ever, and will continue to be part of the right-to-die and euthanasia debate. Unless one believes euthanasia is wrong in every circumstance, the diverse views contributing to the debate can be thought-provoking for anyone trying to make decisions about the morality of euthanasia.

Conflicting Religious Beliefs. Among religious groups that have strict dogma against euthanasia are the Christian Life Commission of the Southern Baptist Convention; the Missouri Synod, a branch of the Lutheran denomination; and a number of nondenominational evangelical churches. Like some Christian groups of the past, these religions teach redemptive suffering—that God sends suffering as a means of washing away people's sins and saving their souls. It is believed that people can be "blessed" if they endure their misery.

A similar belief is part of Islam, a religion based on the teachings of the Prophet Muhammad, who lived during the seventh century and whose followers are known as Muslims. According to Islamic doctrine, illness and suffering are a result of God's will. Taking life for any reason is prohibited. "We don't own ourselves. We are entrusted to God and the taking of life is the right of the one who gives it," noted Hassan Hathout, a California physician who also oversees the outreach program of the Islamic Center of Southern California.[3]

The major Eastern religions of Hinduism and Buddhism are based on diverse teachings and traditions and include varied sects and schools of thought. But both religions basically teach that suffering must be endured. Suffering allows a religious follower to work out her or his karma, or the consequences of deeds committed in a past life. Creeds of both religions also state that people can be reborn again and again, and joys or sorrows come about because of past actions. Most Hindus and Buddhists believe that people who deliberately shorten their life will not be able to repay debts owed for past bad behavior or improve their karma in preparation for the next rebirth.

Hindu and Buddhist views on voluntary euthanasia are subject to many different interpretations, and in some instances ethical codes regarding suicide have been supplanted by military principles. For example, although Japan is a Buddhist country, from medieval times to the twentieth century Japanese warriors sometimes committed hara-kiri (ritual suicide) to avoid capture. During World War II, Japanese pilots deliberately crashed planes loaded with explosives into U.S. and Allied warships, destroying themselves along with their targets. In their suicidal attacks, the kamikaze pilots, as they were called, were carrying out what some may have believed was a divine mission to save the Japanese empire. (*Kamikaze* means "divine wind" in Japanese and was a name given to a typhoon in the thirteenth century that saved the empire by destroying an attacking enemy.) Whatever the kamikaze pilots' belief about the sacredness of their mission, they also were complying with demands of the Japanese emperor, who had strong military control over the entire country.

Although a large number of religious groups today oppose active euthanasia—deliberately ending a life—many nevertheless condone the idea of withholding burdensome medical treatment, or extraordinary life support, from the terminally ill. All branches of Judaism, for example, assert that there is no justification for active euthanasia, but that it is acceptable to avoid measures that would delay death. For centuries the Roman Catholic Church has opposed active euthanasia but has condoned withdrawal of treatment that provides no relief or cure for a terminally ill patient.

Only a few religious groups have considered or issued statements in recent years that favor a person's right to control his or her death. In 1988, the Unitarian Universalist Association, one of the most liberal religious groups in the United States, adopted a resolution on "The Right to Die with Dignity," which calls for a person's right to die "in accordance with one's own choice." In 1991, the United Church of Christ issued a statement that calls for the Church to support right-to-die decisions of families and individuals, including medical assistance in dying if needed.[4]

Views of Health Care Professionals and Families. An estimated 70 percent of the 6,000 deaths that occur daily in the United States are the result of people privately

A Japanese kamikaze pilot flies a suicide mission against an American escort carrier in the western Pacific during World War II.

agreeing to withdraw some life-support mechanism or to not use any death-delaying technology in the first place.[5] At the same time, on any given day, an estimated 10,000 patients remain in vegetative comas in the United States, according to medical experts. The oldest has been in a coma since 1951. Total annual costs to care for patients in vegetative comas are estimated to range from $120 million to $1.2 billion.[6]

Yet the costs of caring for people who appear to be comatose seem of little consequence if a patient recovers. Many doctors can cite examples of patients who appear to experience "miraculous" recoveries despite a prognosis for an imminent death. One case deemed hopeless with no more than one chance in a million of recovery was that of Jackie Cole, a Baltimore, Maryland, woman. Her husband, Harry Cole, a Presbyterian minister, told the family's story in a book titled *One in a Million*.

At age forty-three, Jackie suffered a stroke, with massive bleeding in the brain. Doctors did not expect her to live for more than two days. But with the aid of life-support systems she continued to survive in a comatose state, and for weeks Harry Cole and Jackie's children by a former marriage were faced with a wrenching decision: Should they seek court permission to have Jackie's life-support systems removed?

Jackie had often told her family that she did not want to be kept alive by artificial means, and had said just before she lost consciousness that she did not want to live "that way"—hooked up to machines. Although Jackie's family wanted to abide by her request to "pull the plug" if her case seemed hopeless, they could not do so without permission of a circuit court judge.

When Harry Cole went to court on Jackie's behalf, the judge denied his petition to withdraw life support. Then, six days later, Jackie awoke from her coma. Over the weeks and months that followed she slowly began to recover from her stroke.

Jackie's case "muddied the waters surrounding a person's right to die," wrote Harry Cole. But he pointed out that his wife's amazing recovery did not change his or Jackie's "basic belief that an individual has the right to determine his or her medical treatment, including the choice to terminate artificial life supports that do not heal but only postpone death." According to Harry, Jackie has repeatedly stated that she approved her family's decision. She said she "would have done the same thing" if she had been in their place.[7]

The American Medical Association (AMA) frequently has issued statements on withdrawing medical treatment at the request of a terminally ill patient and also on the much-debated question of when it is justifiable to stop life-support measures for a person judged to be in a persistent vegetative state. In 1989, the AMA Council on Scientific Affairs and Council on Ethical and Judicial Affairs published their collective viewpoint, which stated:

> *For humane reasons, with informed consent, a physician may do what is medically necessary to alleviate severe pain, or cease or omit treatment to permit a terminally ill patient to die when death is imminent. . . . Even if death is not imminent but a patient is beyond doubt permanently unconscious . . . it is not unethical to discontinue all means of life-prolonging medical treatment . . . [which] includes medication and artificially or technologically supplied respiration, nutrition or hydration.*[8]

The majority of physicians and other health care professionals and most bioethicists agree with this position, but they have very different views about assisted suicide and active euthanasia. Assisted suicide is not uncommon among physicians treating terminally ill patients, according to a group of twelve doctors who jointly prepared an article on euthanasia for the *New England Journal of Medicine*. The article pointed out that many doctors believe assisted suicide "is the last act in a continuum of care provided for the hopelessly ill patient." All but two of the writers said they themselves believed "it is not immoral for a physician to assist in the rational suicide of a terminally ill person." But in their opinion, the majority of U.S. physicians apparently do not favor active euthanasia—performing a medical procedure that directly causes death.[9]

Many physicians say they would be clouding their roles as healers if they helped patients to die. They could never accept the idea of being both a healer and a killer. Health care professionals and ethicists maintain that physicians are obligated to practice according to the ancient Greek Hippocratic Oath. In taking this oath, a physician promises to help the sick and never to cause harm.

Yet medical students today do not necessarily take the oath, and some scholars believe the oath is outdated and open to a variety of interpretations. For example, some believe medical practitioners may cause harm to patients if they withhold high doses of pain-killing drugs that could also hasten death.

Some health care professionals say they are convinced that calls for doctor-assisted suicide and euthanasia are really expressions of frustration or despair. People are trying to take control of their own deaths or are seeking help for family members who are dying in agony. "I've seen patients rocking in bed, in terrible pain—it doesn't seem like something God could want. Medical technology can save a life, but the life isn't always worth living out," a bioethicist teaching at St. Thomas University in Miami, Florida, told a local news reporter in 1992.[10]

Frustration and despair were evident in the case of the Linares family of Chicago. Fifteen-month-old Sammy Linares had accidentally swallowed a piece of a balloon, which obstructed his breathing. As a result, he had been comatose for months and was not expected to recover. He was connected to life-support systems in Rush-Presbyterian-St. Luke's Medical Center. The Linares family had requested that Sammy be allowed to die, but the hospital had no legal precedent at that time (1989) for terminating the life of a minor and asked the family to seek a court order.

Rudy Linares, Sammy's father, was so distraught that he was determined to remove his son from the life-support systems. One day he rushed into the hospital armed with a .357 Magnum. Although hospital staff tried to restrain Linares, he held them off at gunpoint. Linares disconnected the machines, picked up his son and cradled him in his arms until there was no question that the little boy was dead. Then Rudy Linares surrendered quietly to police.

Linares was charged with murder, but a grand jury refused to indict him because the medical examiner did not state that the child's death was a homicide. There was an outpouring of public sympathy for the Linares family, with letters and calls coming from across the nation. A teenager wrote:

> *I am a 17-year-old boy who suffers from cerebral palsy. Because of a birth defect my first two months of life were spent on a life support system. I was greatly moved and angered by the Rudy Linares tragedy. In an incident of pure love for*

The obvious and public anguish of Rudy Linares, accused of killing his fifteen-month-old son by disconnecting him from a life-support system, moved many people to acknowledge their support of his actions.

*his son a man is charged with murder. The state
law that allows such a charge is in fact the true
criminal, not Mr. Linares, who acted out of love
for his own son.* [11]

Linares was later charged and found guilty of illegally
carrying a weapon and sentenced to a year of probation.
The case prompted the state of Illinois to set up a task
force of medical, legal, and religious experts who later
became advisers for the Park Ridge Center for the Study of
Health, Faith, and Ethics. Part of their mission is to establish ethical and legal guidelines that could be used when
requests are made to withdraw life support from terminally ill patients.

Assisted Suicide
and Active Euthanasia

Dozens of national and regional polls conducted over the past decade show consistently that most Americans favor some form of euthanasia. More than 60 percent of those polled said doctors should be allowed to ease suffering and end a patient's life in a painless way at the request of the patient.

In 1991, the *Boston Globe* and the Harvard School of Public Health sponsored a national telephone survey of 1,311 adults to determine views on euthanasia. Results of the poll revealed that "64 percent of Americans favor physician-assisted suicide and euthanasia for terminally ill patients who request it." According to the newspaper report, people fear "a lingering and painful death on medical life-support systems, and most people do not seem troubled by proposals for more permissive policies on physician-assisted dying." But only 37 percent of the respondents felt that relatives or friends of the dying should be allowed to perform the deed, and only 14 percent would want to take such steps themselves.

According to Brown University ethicist Dan Brock, the findings make sense because "We would like to restrict the authority [to perform euthanasia] to some group we can oversee . . . and whose professional training and norms lead us to think they're less likely to abuse it. And doctors have the technical expertise to make sure it is being done only in the appropriate circumstances."[1]

Assisted suicide is prohibited in more than half of the states, however, and active euthanasia is illegal nationwide. A number of right-to-die groups across the nation are trying to change restrictive laws and pass "death with dignity" acts, a topic covered in Chapter 6. Meantime, with prohibitions still in place, some people will defy laws or circumvent them because they believe it is morally right to help a hopelessly ill person die. Others say in no uncertain terms that assisted suicide is murder.

Mercy or Murder? Many of those who seek help in ending their lives are people with incurable and agonizing diseases such as acquired immune deficiency syndrome (AIDS), certain severe respiratory ailments, and cancers. In recent years, reports of assisted suicides and euthanasia cases have appeared in newspapers across the continent. For example, David Lewis, an AIDS counselor in Vancouver, British Columbia, revealed in 1990 that he had helped eight male friends with AIDS to take lethal doses of drugs that had been prescribed earlier by a doctor. Lewis said none of the men wanted to suffer anymore and begged to die. "To refuse to help them would be criminal," he said.[2]

Other caregivers working with AIDS patients in the United States have disclosed similar actions. But in an article for the *The New York Times Magazine*, a retired physician described why he could not comply with a request from an AIDS patient for help to die with dignity in his home. The doctor at first agreed to help, but he feared that "the police would ask questions" and he would be implicated. "There would be publicity, the press. It would be vicious," he wrote. He was unable to assist in the act, even though it seemed the patient was near death. (The AIDS patient died weeks later in the intensive-care unit of a hospital.)[3]

A former health care professional in the Pacific Northwest revealed that she came to the aid of her father, who had severe emphysema (a lung disease) and wanted to die. She discussed with her father how much of the medicines already in their house would be fatal. Then the two of them bought liquor to amplify the effect of the drugs. But her father insisted that she leave their home, so that she would not be charged with abetting his suicide.

In a California incident, James Sutherland, twenty-eight, of Fresno, acted on his wife Tina's request for aid in dying. Tina suffered from terminal cancer and was bedridden. While Tina slept, James Sutherland mixed codeine and antidepressant tablets into a solution that he injected into his wife's feeding tube. The deadly mixture killed Tina, and James Sutherland was charged with murder and convicted. But he received a sentence of only one year in jail and five years' probation. According to news accounts, the prosecutor and judge in the case determined that Sutherland acted with no ill intent and meant to effect a peaceful release for his wife. However, Tina's mother did not believe the evidence supported that decision and appealed the case.[4]

The Elderly and Euthanasia. The largest group of Americans who want to determine for themselves how they will die are the elderly, according to federal studies.[5] Some elderly people who are suffering from fatal and intolerable illnesses may plead with their mates or other family members to help them die. One well-publicized case was that of the Gilberts of Fort Lauderdale, Florida.

Emily Gilbert was a victim of Alzheimer's disease, a brain disorder that destroys mental capacities and causes severe physical deterioration. She also suffered a painful bone ailment and had begged many times to die. In 1985, Emily's husband, Roswell Gilbert, believed he was performing an act of mercy when he shot and killed his wife. But a jury found otherwise and convicted Gilbert of first-degree murder. He was sentenced to twenty years in prison, although in 1990 Florida governor Bob Martinez granted clemency, allowing Gilbert to go free.

Another case made headlines in 1990 when Bertram Harper of California agreed to help his wife, Virginia, to commit suicide. Virginia was terminally ill with liver cancer and had planned how and when she wanted to die. But she needed help to carry out her wishes. Since assisted suicide is prohibited in California, the couple decided to travel to Michigan, where the act was not illegal. The Harpers asked Virginia's daughter to go with them.

On the day she planned to die, Virginia took an overdose of sleeping pills and pulled a plastic bag over her head to facilitate her own dying. When she became too warm, her husband and daughter tried to ease her discomfort by lifting the bag several times. Then Bertram Harper pulled the bag down over his wife's face one last time, and Virginia died.

After Virginia's death was reported, prosecutors charged Bertram Harper with second-degree murder on the grounds that Bertram had contributed to the death of another. Prosecutors advised Harper to plead guilty to manslaughter, which would have brought probation and a sentence of community service. Harper refused, because he said "I knew in my heart what I did was right . . . as far as I was concerned I had not committed a crime." But he added that he knew the law might not see it that way.

In May 1991, a jury acquitted Harper. One of the jurors said he and most of the other jurors could put themselves in Harper's shoes and were ready to acquit even before they left the jury box. They concluded that Virginia Harper voluntarily carried out her own plans to commit suicide. Thus the jury determined that Bertram Harper was not a murderer.[6]

Doctor-Assisted Suicide and Euthanasia. In spite of Dr. Timothy Quill's account describing how he aided a leukemia patient, few other doctors would admit publicly that they have assisted in suicides. Neither would most doctors announce publicly that they have administered lethal doses of drugs to dying patients in order to alleviate suffering and shorten the dying process. In the few instances over the past decade in which doctors reported participating in euthanasia, most were charged with murder but were not convicted.

However, a stormy legal and ethical controversy broke out when Jack Kevorkian of Michigan made no secret of helping three seriously ill patients to commit suicide. Kevorkian was a retired pathologist and also a trained physician, although he had not practiced medicine. In 1990, Kevorkian helped Janet Adkins, from Portland, Oregon, to end her life.

Adkins was a victim of early Alzheimer's and had indicated to her husband, other family members, and friends that she wanted to plan her death while she was still mentally competent. She and her husband were members of the Hemlock Society. In 1989, Janet Adkins heard about Dr. Kevorkian and a machine he had invented that would allow terminally ill patients to end their lives. Kevorkian had developed the device for a research project, and he hoped to publish the results in a medical journal. When Janet Adkins first contacted Kevorkian by telephone, he refused to assist in her suicide and convinced her to try an experimental drug treatment for Alzheimer's disease.

After six months the treatment had no effect, and Janet contacted Kevorkian again. Her husband, Ron, and her physician also spoke with him, explaining her wishes. This time Kevorkian agreed to help. Ron and Janet Adkins flew to Michigan so that Janet could end her life with what was later dubbed the "suicide machine."

The device has since been shown countless times on television and in magazine and newspaper photos. It consisted of three glass bottles that hung inside a frame and were connected to an intravenous (IV) tube that was inserted into Janet's arm. One bottle contained a saline solution, the second a sedative, and the third potassium chloride, which is lethal. Janet pushed a button to activate the flow of solution, which first sedated her and then eventually caused her death.

After Adkins's death, Kevorkian was arrested and charged with murder. But the judge dismissed the case on the grounds that Michigan had no law against doctor-assisted suicide.

Once the suicide was reported, however, public reaction—both pro and con—was swift and explosive. The controversy became even more intense when, in the fall of 1991, Kevorkian assisted in the deaths of two other seriously ill women who wanted to die: Sherry Miller, who suffered from multiple sclerosis, and Marjorie Wantz, who had a painful pelvic disease. Both women were from Michigan. Kevorkian provided Miller with carbon monoxide, a lethal gas, which she inhaled through a mask. Wantz used a version of Kevorkian's suicide machine. Kevorkian immediately reported the deaths.

About a month later, in November 1991, the State Board of Medicine revoked Kevorkian's medical license. Then, in December, the deaths of the two women were

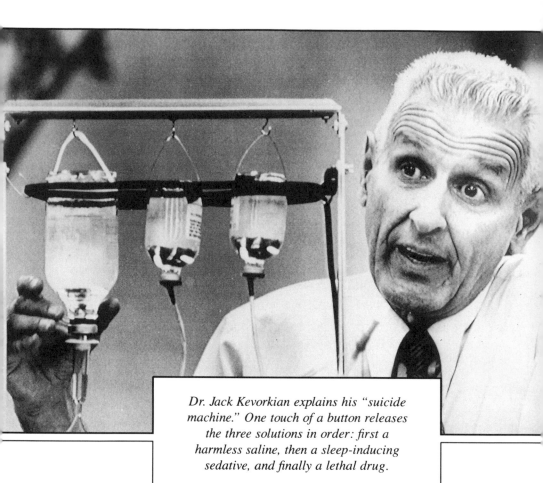

Dr. Jack Kevorkian explains his "suicide machine." One touch of a button releases the three solutions in order: first a harmless saline, then a sleep-inducing sedative, and finally a lethal drug.

ruled homicides. In February 1992, Kevorkian was charged with murder, and a jury trial was scheduled for the fall.

Meantime, though, in May 1992, Kevorkian helped another Michigan woman, Susan Williams, find the means to commit suicide with self-administered carbon monoxide. Williams suffered from severe multiple sclerosis and was blind. According to a police report, Kevorkian was with the woman when she died but was not charged with assisting in Williams's use of the deadly gas.[7]

In July 1992, Circuit Court Judge David Breck dismissed first-degree murder charges against Kevorkian in the deaths of Miller and Wantz. Once again, as in the Adkins case, charges were dropped because physician-assisted suicide was not a crime in Michigan. However, Richard Thompson, the Oakland County prosecutor who brought the murder charges, said he would appeal the decision, and he, along with some other Michigan officials, called for the state legislature to enact a law making assisted suicide a felony.

In November 1992, Kevorkian assisted in the suicide of a sixth woman in Michigan. The very next day, the Michigan House of Representatives passed a bill making assisted suicide a felony punishable by four years in prison. The state Senate also passed the bill; the law went into effect in February 1993.

Critics and Supporters. Those opposing Kevorkian's actions frequently argued that the women who committed suicide were not terminally ill and that society is obligated to find other alternatives for those who need relief from agonizing disabilities. Many detractors nicknamed Kevorkian "Dr. Death" or called him a ghoul. Reacting to Janet Adkins's suicide, Arthur Caplan, director of the Center for Biomedical Ethics at the University of Minnesota, wrote:

> *Kevorkian helped kill someone whom he says he met for the first time two days earlier. After explaining his machine to Mrs. Adkins over din-*

ner, he apparently decided she was competent to make the choice to kill herself.

This is, to be polite, a moral outrage. Kevorkian is a pathologist, not a psychologist or psychiatrist. He has limited experience in dealing with living patients. His stock in trade was examining dead ones. Could he really be confident that Janet Adkins really wanted to die, based upon two days of personal contact?[8]

Other critics contended that a great many citizens were repulsed by Kevorkian's actions and believed he should be convicted of murder. Right-to-life groups generally supported a murder indictment for Kevorkian; they believe that doctor-assisted suicide is killing.

Of those defending Kevorkian, two were friends of Wantz and Miller and were with the women when they died. They hoped the case against Kevorkian would clear the way for doctors to help those who want to die.

Apparently many others shared this view, according to a *Detroit Free Press* survey. The poll included a random sampling of 310 people across Michigan and an extra sampling of 102 people in Oakland County, where Kevorkian's case was heard. By a margin of five to one, respondents statewide said they did not believe Kevorkian was a murderer, and in Oakland County the margin was ten to one in favor of acquitting Kevorkian of murder charges. Some were convinced that Kevorkian was breaking new ground and that he was "fighting for everyone's personal freedom."

One woman who was interviewed thought officials were making a scapegoat of Kevorkian. Others said they believed the prosecution of Kevorkian was motivated by religious beliefs rather than any legal prohibition, since there was no Michigan law against assisted suicide. As one

"SUICIDE DEVICE" INVENTOR ADDS TO HIS CREDENTIALS...

JACK
KEVORKIAN

M.D.

PATHOLOGIST

GOD

ROTHCO

As this cartoon eloquently expresses,
critics of physician-assisted suicide
believe that doctors like Jack Kevorkian
are doing nothing less than playing God.

respondent put it: "Jesus himself had a form of suicide. All he would have had to do to stop it is say the word."9

Across the nation public reactions after Kevorkian's indictment were consistent with previous polls: Although the majority favored assisted suicide and euthanasia in certain cases, some were adamantly opposed to any type of active euthanasia. The *Atlanta Constitution* reported, for example, that in the opinion of one Georgia couple euthanasia seemed on the surface to be a "loving thing to do, but the ramifications of any legalized killing are just beyond what this society should tolerate. . . . The right to die can quickly become the duty to die."

On the other hand, an elderly Atlanta woman supported the idea of mercy killing: "Both my father and husband's father lived about five years beyond being able to recognize anybody. . . . They weren't really alive. I feel like it's time to permit people to die with dignity. . . . We ought to be able to control our death as much as we control the rest of our lives."

A heart transplant patient who also needed a kidney transplant favored the idea of "helping yourself out of this world easily, if you can. I myself am going to die shortly. . . . The prospect of lying around and dying a slow death just isn't attractive at all."10

In a letter to the *Washington Times*, one man wrote: "God bless Dr. Jack Kevorkian! By helping several people suffering from unbearable and incurable illnesses to commit suicide, he has shown that he is far more interested in alleviating human suffering than most doctors . . . [who] seem to be interested only in keeping patients breathing, regardless of how much they are suffering."11

Kevorkian's Views. What did Kevorkian have to say? In a number of interviews, he explained that he did not believe he had ever caused a death, but rather had helped people exercise their "last civil right." He accused physicians who oppose euthanasia and assisted suicide of being similar to the Nazi doctors who tortured and conducted experiments on Holocaust victims. In Kevorkian's view it is the same as torture not to help people who are in excruciating pain to die if they so choose. [12]

Kevorkian said repeatedly that he was concerned about the "suffering humanity out there," and that a prison sentence would be small punishment compared to what some extremely ill patients undergo. In a book published in 1991 he explained how he came to believe in euthanasia and assisted suicide. During his first year in medical internship, he witnessed the ravaging effects of cancer on a middle-aged woman. Kevorkian described her as:

> *helplessly immobile . . . her entire body jaundiced to an intense yellow-brown, skin stretched paper-thin over a fluid-filled abdomen swollen to four or five times normal size. The rest of her was an emaciated skeleton: sagging, discolored skin covered her bones like a cheap, wrinkled frock.*
>
> *The poor wretch stared up at me. . . . It seemed as though she was pleading for help and death at the same time. Out of sheer empathy alone I could have helped her die with satisfaction. From that moment on, I was sure that doctor-assisted euthanasia and suicide are and always were ethical, no matter what anyone says or thinks.* [13]

"Self-Deliverance." As a member of the Hemlock Society, Janet Adkins believed in "self-deliverance," or being able to choose her own manner of death. She opted for suicide with the assistance of Jack Kevorkian. But the Hemlock Society itself does not support Kevorkian. Even though the group promotes the right of the terminally ill to make choices on whether they will prolong their lives, it does not encourage suicide in the absence of terminal illness. Since Dr. Kevorkian's patients were not facing imminent death, the society does not defend Kevorkian's actions, according to Cheryl Smith, a staff attorney at the society's headquarters in Eugene, Oregon. She added, however, that Kevorkian has prompted at least one positive reaction: a national debate on the subject of assisted suicide.[14]

Derek Humphry, who founded the society in 1980 and retired in mid-1992, believes that laws prohibiting assisted suicide are archaic and should be changed. In fact, one purpose of the Hemlock Society is to campaign for passage of laws that would allow physicians to help terminally ill patients die.

Humphry has written a number of books that explain how dying people can end their suffering, including actual cases of assisted suicide. Humphry's best-selling book *Final Exit*, published in 1991, is basically a manual on how to commit a "responsible suicide," complete with detailed instructions on administering fatal doses of prescription drugs.

Membership in the Hemlock Society has been increasing steadily over the years, but critics of the group and its founder are numerous, too. Among them is Leon R. Kass, a University of Chicago professor and trained physician. In a scathing criticism of *Final Exit*, Kass called the book "evil," declaring that it "should never have been written." He labeled Derek Humphry the "Lord High Executioner" and maintained that Humphry used "sloppy reasoning" in his arguments for doctor-assisted suicide.

Kass also said that advice in the book could encourage suicide among the physically disabled and the depressed—people who could be helped to live productive lives.

Well aware of the "horrors" caused unintentionally as medical practitioners attempt to ward off death, Kass did note, "There are many, many circumstances . . . that call for the cessation of medical intervention." He also advocated proper doses of medication to ease the pain of terminally ill patients, even if that hastens death. Practitioners can do much more "to support the morale and dignity of people faced with incurable or fatal illness. But to cross the line and accept active euthanasia . . . that way lies madness." He warned that there are those "who stand ready in the wings to exploit the 'choice' for death, to make sure that the burdensome and incurable take advantage of the deadly option."[15]

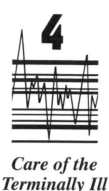

Care of the
Terminally Ill

An increasing number of caregivers believe that easing or managing pain, along with treating the psychological and spiritual needs of patients, can help reduce demands for assisted suicide or "mercy killing." Unfortunately, few physicians are highly trained in pain management, since knowledge about techniques and education on this subject have been available for only a relatively short time. Many doctors and their patients have feared the use of high doses of opioid drugs (such as morphine), for example, because of concerns that such treatment would lead to addiction.

Some patients, such as those with cancer, do become dependent on pain medication. When they no longer need pain relief, they may have to be weaned from a drug to prevent withdrawal symptoms. But that "is very different from addiction or psychological dependence . . . [on] drug use characterized by continual craving for the opioid with compulsive drug-seeking behavior," according to Dr. Kathleen M. Foley of the Memorial Sloan-Kettering Cancer Center in New York.

At the Pain Clinic, Dr. Foley often sees patients whose uncontrolled pain leads them to consider suicide or to ask doctors to help them to die. When patients believe no relief is available, they feel helpless and anxious, which amplifies the pain and the death wish. In contrast, patients who know that a cure is possible can tolerate a great deal of pain. With a combination of drugs, surgery, and psychological support, physicians can help patients achieve some comfort and lessen or eliminate suicidal tendencies. Foley believes that many more physicians and other caregivers must be trained to minimize patient distress.[1]

Susan Tolle, director of the Ethics Center at the Oregon Health Sciences University, agrees. In a speech before a Portland civic group, Tolle said that at least two thirds of dying patients who need relief from pain do not receive adequate pain medication. She acknowledged that physicians have been concerned about the possibility of drug addiction among patients, but said this concern appears to make little sense when patients are dying and suffering. However, medical practitioners are still reluctant to use large doses of pain-killing drugs, because if these drugs shorten life, they fear "the possibility of litigation, public scrutiny, or [adverse] professional judgment," Tolle said.

Yet the primary responsibility of physicians, nurses, and other health care providers is to meet the needs of suffering patients. Tolle, along with a growing number of other professional caregivers, believes in more effective palliative care. The goal of palliative medicine is not to cure but to ease pain and suffering for those who will soon die. "It is often difficult for the medical profession to make the transition from curative treatment to palliative care," in Tolle's opinion. But physicians can provide pain management, comfort, and support. She recommended more full use of hospice programs that provide continuing care for dying patients.[2]

The Hospice Approach. The hospice idea of providing compassionate care and comfort for the dying has a long history. The term was used in medieval times to describe a place of shelter for tired or sick travelers. Today *hospice* refers to a special kind of care and support for people in the final stages of a terminal illness. This concept of special care developed with the work of Cicely Saunders in Great Britain during the late 1960s.

Saunders, who was a nurse during World War II, was concerned about the lack of treatment provided for terminally ill patients. At the time, British doctors tending patients in hospitals often were evasive about terminal illness and tried to sidestep visits with those who were dying. Unless private nurses or other caregivers were available, many people died alone. Determined to change this approach, Saunders returned to medical school and became a physician.

In 1967, Saunders opened the Saint Christopher's Hospice outside London. Over the years thousands of people have chosen to spend their last months, weeks, or days in the hospice in order to die "a good death," without artificial life supports.[3]

A basic philosophy for the hospice movement in the United States emerged along with the ideas of psychiatrist Elisabeth Kubler-Ross. In the late 1960s, she began to conduct seminars on confronting death in a realistic but sensitive manner. Her book *On Death and Dying* and others that followed have been required reading for many death counselors and those who teach courses in dealing with death.

Kubler-Ross helped people cope with their fears of death. She led the dying on a "journey" through what she called the five stages of death. These begin with denial and anger over one's impending death and move on to bargaining for longer life, then depression, and finally acceptance of the inevitable.

Cicely Saunders, the British physician credited with developing the concept of hospice, wanted to help people die confidently rather than fearfully.

Helping people accept death is part of the hospice approach in the United States. The first U.S. hospice facility opened in Connecticut in 1974. Since then almost 1,800 hospice programs have been set up across the United States, providing services so that terminally ill patients can remain at home or in a homelike setting and live as fully as possible until death.

People sometimes mistakenly view the hospice approach to dying as euthanasia or "mercy killing." But the National Hospice Organization in Washington, D.C., opposes legalization of euthanasia, aid-in-dying, and physician-assisted suicide. The organization stated:

> *Hospice recognizes dying as part of the normal process of living and focuses on maintaining the quality of remaining life. Hospice affirms life and neither hastens nor postpones death. Hospice exists in the hope and belief that through appropriate care and the promotion of a caring community sensitive to their needs, patients and families may be free to obtain a degree of mental and spiritual preparation for death that is satisfactory to them.*[4]

Some hospice programs operate within a section of a hospital or in a separate continuing care center, or nursing home. Other programs provide volunteers and nurses who visit patients in their homes. If hospice care takes place in a patient's home, a nurse may visit to offer pain-control medication or help with medical equipment. A home health care aide may bathe a patient or help with other personal services. A member of the clergy might provide counseling, and a volunteer might visit to relieve the primary caregiver for a few hours. Volunteers and clergy also

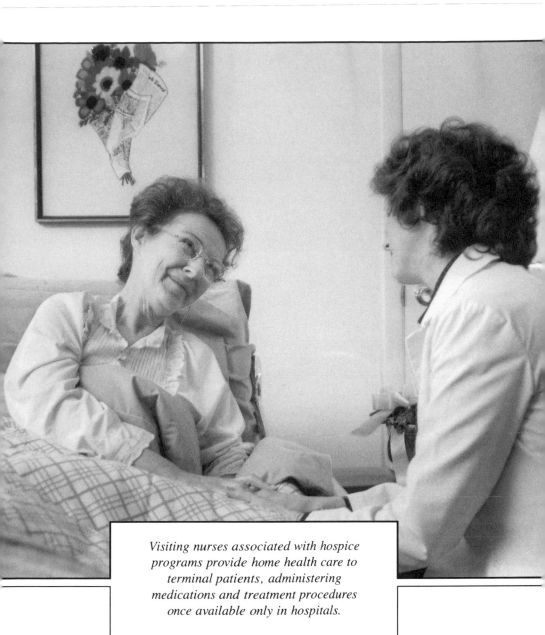

*Visiting nurses associated with hospice
programs provide home health care to
terminal patients, administering
medications and treatment procedures
once available only in hospitals.*

help family members cope and grieve after the death of a loved one.

Objections to Hospice Care. Of course, not all terminally ill patients want hospice care. Some may request that medical practitioners try every means possible to bring about a cure. Others choose to die at home but do not need hospice because they are cared for by family members and friends. Still others find hospice offers poor quality or inconsistent care.

In an article published in *Health* magazine, Vicki Brower described what she termed "abysmal care" provided for her terminally ill mother, who opted to remain at home. Brower's mother had incurable lung cancer and occasionally needed oxygen and other medical intervention to ease extreme breathing difficulties.

When Brower enrolled her mother in a hospice program, she asked whether a doctor would be called if needed to perform a surgical tap to drain fluid from her mother's lungs. The hospice nurse could see no reason for the procedure and felt it would only prolong life. In the nurse's opinion, Brower's mother had not fully accepted that she would die, and thus was probably not a good candidate for the hospice program. Brower maintained that her mother was always "feisty" and wanted to live out her life; no one had the right to decide what her "appropriate" behavior should be.

Although Brower and her mother entered the program, the experience was difficult. Two years after her mother's death, Brower wrote: "My mother and I repeatedly faced criticism, indifference and even negligence, stemming from the same attitude the intake nurse had shown—the idea that Mom should just embrace death quietly and peacefully."

Brower charged that some in the hospice movement believe "there is one and only one right way to die. In my mother's case, for example, it was apparently 'right' for her to calmly accept the news that she was supposed to die within six months and to gasp for breath without expecting medical treatment because she was going to die soon anyway."[5] Such rigid approaches are not typical of hospice, as Brower pointed out. But others share her complaints and contend that some patients do not receive enough relief from pain.

On the other hand, some hospice workers believe that patients may not be allowed to die peacefully because family members pressure for medical intervention. Or physicians may be "incredibly aggressive" and "invasive" when treating dying patients in hospice, according to a Portland, Oregon, hospice worker with eighteen years of experience. The worker accused some doctors of making immoral decisions on the basis of how much they can bill for treatment, such as ordering expensive kidney dialysis when a patient has only about twelve hours left to live.[6]

Yet as Susan Tolle argued, aggressive treatment may result because of the inability of doctors to stand by and passively watch a patient die. They "can't let go, can't see that it's time to shift gears," she explained. "When the patient says it's time to quit because there's no more hope, the doctor is unable to say: 'I can't cure you, but there's a whole lot my friends in the hospice can do.' It's an incredible transition and some physicians can never make it."[7]

The "Hospice Six." Because hospice care is designed to enable patients to live without pain during the dying process, physicians prescribe pain-killing drugs that nurses administer when needed. But easing the pain of terminally ill patients turned into a traumatic ordeal for six nurses at the Hospice of St. Peter's Community Hospital in Helena, Montana.

The story began in late 1989 with a practice that to many in the small community of 25,000 seemed a minor infraction, a bit of fudging on the law to show mercy to those in extreme pain. Families of deceased patients gave leftover pain medication (morphine) to the nurses in the hospice, which is located two blocks from the hospital. Although laws require that health care workers destroy unused drugs left when patients die, the nurses kept the painkillers, storing them in an unlocked desk drawer at the hospice.

Senior nurse Mary Mouat and other hospice nurses knew from past experience that pain medication was not always available when patients needed it, and one hour in extreme pain can be an eternity to a suffering person. State law requires a written prescription for each new supply of morphine, but doctors might not be available to write the prescriptions and pharmacies might be closed. So for about a year, the nurses used the leftover drugs to treat other hopelessly ill patients in emergency situations.

Several nurses related instances of patients writhing in pain, when the only way to relieve the torture was to administer morphine from the illicit stockpile of drugs. Patients usually had earlier prescriptions for the drugs on file or had previously taken similar pain-killing medications. All the patients receiving morphine had signed legal documents stating that medication should be administered to alleviate suffering, even though it might hasten death.

An investigation into these practices began in 1991 after a nurse on the hospital staff (not connected with hospice treatment) complained to supervisors. The state's professional licensing bureau threatened to revoke or suspend the nurses' licenses. Steven Shapiro, legal counsel for the state, said the nurses had mishandled drugs and had violated their professional ethics code. He declared that the drug laws were passed to protect the public and patients from potential dangers of misuse. Morphine kept in an unlocked drawer could pose a great public risk, he contended.

Shapiro accused the nurses of shortening lives and told reporters that the state did not condone giving high doses of medication if such treatment brought an early death. "The doctors and nurses have to find their limits. At some point, there is nothing more to be done. It's unfortunate . . . some people are going to suffer," he said. The executive director of the state's board of nursing agreed with Shapiro and said that sometimes a more appropriate procedure would be holding a dying patient's hand rather than giving heavy doses of painkillers.

Defense lawyers for the nurses, and the hospital administrator, countered that what the hospice nurses did was common practice and that there was no evidence of harm. The hospice's former medical director said he had "given injections of morphine knowing it could stop a patient's breathing. It's the right of the patient to determine whether to control the pain or extend life." In the doctor's opinion withholding painkillers was unethical.

Hundreds of people were outraged that caregivers would be required to withhold medication that would relieve a dying person's agony. Letters and phone calls came from people in the community and across the nation. Hospice nurses in other cities said they had done what the Helena nurses had done or would follow that practice without qualms. Many people who had seen loved ones die in hospice care supported the nurses. One letter-writer thought the nurses deserved a Distinguished Service Award.

Lawyer Shapiro and the nursing board, however, were more concerned about abiding by the law—dotting every "i" and crossing every "t", as the hospital administrator put it. Shapiro said it was his job to enforce the law and not to address the issue of compassionate care for dying patients. The nursing board placed the six nurses on probation for three to five years. The nurses also were required to complete additional education classes on hospice policy and procedures and patient care and to document their work. If they violated the order, their licenses could be suspended.

How did the nurses react? All felt they had acted properly toward their patients even though they had bent the rules to do so. None believed their actions were wrong. But they all felt the case created a terrible stigma.

Supervisor Mary Mouat resigned her position and took a non-nursing job. Three other nurses also left the hospice, one moving out of state. Of the two that remained at the hospice, one, Alene Brackman, said, "For the first time in the 30 years that I've been a nurse, I'm thinking about my license before I think about my patient." She hoped that the case would generate new hospital policies and emergency plans for taking care of dying patients' needs in a humane way.[8]

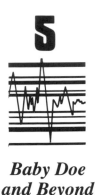

Baby Doe and Beyond

A child is born. For a vast majority of families, it is a joyous event. But for some parents and health care professionals, the birth of a child with severe disabilities or the premature birth of a tiny (less than two pounds) infant ushers in a host of medical, ethical, and legal issues and emotional traumas.

One of the most pressing questions is whether physicians should take aggressive action to keep severely impaired babies alive, or whether such babies should be allowed to die. Do parents have the right to make that decision for their child and refuse medical treatment? Do physicians have the right to overrule parents in life-and-death matters? Should such matters be brought before the courts?

There are also questions about who should pay the exorbitant costs of trying to save the lives of damaged babies or fragile, low-birthweight babies who cannot survive without extraordinary treatment, such as twenty-four-hour care and the use of expensive medical equipment. Before the 1980s, a baby weighing one and a half pounds rarely survived. Today, nearly half the infants weighing a little over one pound survive due to advanced medical technology. But the majority suffer neurological damage, and keeping such an infant alive may cost more than $2,000 per day, not to mention the emotional costs that parents must bear. [1]

Many people ask: Is it morally right to continue care for severely damaged and dying babies in intensive-care units (units that are understaffed in some hospitals) if other babies with a greater chance for a healthy survival do not receive adequate care? What about the continued costs and caregiving required if a child is born brain-damaged and physically handicapped? Should physicians do everything in their power to treat premature and impaired infants even if their chances for survival are slim? In the 1980s, a case known in court as "Baby Doe" (to protect the privacy of the family) called attention to these questions and focused also on the terrible dilemma of deciding whether to prolong the life of an impaired infant or to let the child die.

Baby Doe. Baby Doe, a boy, was born in 1982 in a Bloomington, Indiana, hospital. He had Down syndrome, which causes a form of mental retardation usually recognized at once by facial characteristics common to most sufferers. The baby's esophagus also was malformed. Anything given by mouth was liable to end up in the baby's lungs, causing suffocation. Following usual procedures, the obstetrician on the case, Dr. Walter Owens, consulted with other doctors about the course of treatment.

Two pediatricians recommended that the baby be transferred immediately to a hospital in nearby Indianapolis. They thought Baby Doe should undergo corrective surgery on the esophagus. But two other doctors supported Owens's view that the surgery might not be successful and of course would have no effect on the baby's mental retardation. They also agreed with Owens that Baby Doe should stay in the Bloomington Hospital and be kept comfortable until death occurred.

As required by law, parents (or guardians) have to consent to any form of medical treatment for their child. In this case, the parents decided to accept Owens's recommended procedure, believing that since their child would be severely mentally retarded they were acting in his best interests. Because some doctors disagreed with Owens and the baby's parents, the hospital management intervened and asked the county court judge to call an emergency hearing.

The judge concluded that Baby Doe's parents had the right to make an informed decision about the course of treatment for their child as recommended by their doctor. Welfare officials could have appealed the ruling but decided against it. However, the county prosecutor appealed to the Indiana Supreme Court. When the judges allowed the lower court ruling to stand, the prosecutor's office attempted to get an emergency hearing from the U.S. Supreme Court. But Baby Doe died, five days after he was born.

The Aftermath. The Baby Doe case generated editorials of outrage in major newspapers and magazines across the nation. Writers reproached the Indiana courts for allowing a helpless infant to starve to death. Well-known columnist George Will, who is the father of a Down syndrome child, accused infant Doe's parents of being inhumane and treating their child and people like him as less than human. Right-to-life activists and handicapped people and their advocates proclaimed that the baby should have been saved. And President Ronald Reagan and some members of his administration, including Surgeon General C. Everett Koop, said that actions in the Baby Doe case were discriminatory. The administration claimed that refusing surgery for the infant was a violation of a federal law prohibiting discrimination against the handicapped (section 504 of the Rehabilitation Act of 1973).

Within a year, the Department of Health and Human Services issued regulations, informally known as "Baby Doe Guidelines," that had to be posted in hospitals accepting federal funds. The guidelines spelled out the federal statute that prohibits discrimination. They also stated that "Any person having knowledge that a handicapped infant is being discriminatorily denied food or customary medical care should immediately contact" the U.S. Department of Health and Human Services by calling a toll-free number. People were urged to get in touch with a state child protective agency as well.

The American Medical Association, the American Academy of Pediatrics, the National Association of Children's Hospitals, and other groups were adamantly opposed to the regulations. Medical officials pointed out that under these rules doctors would be required to prolong lives even when infants were born with truly hopeless conditions.

These conditions include anencephaly, in which an infant is born without a brain or with only part of a brain. Although most brain-absent infants die at birth or a few days later, modern technology could keep such babies biologically alive for weeks or perhaps longer. Another condition considered hopeless is severe bleeding in the head, which leads to severe brain damage and requires continual use of a respirator. Another condition, in which an infant is born without a major portion of the intestines, cannot be treated by surgery. Such a baby can be kept alive by injecting nutritional fluids into the bloodstream, but the treatment only prolongs dying.

Physicians argued that attempting to keep an infant alive under such conditions was useless and brought hardship and pain to families. Medical professionals also were opposed to a federal ruling that allowed federal officials to go into hospitals to investigate the condition of newborns. Because of this practice, some doctors spent hours in futile attempts to revive babies born with extreme abnormalities. To do otherwise might have resulted in criminal prosecution.

George J. Annas, professor of Health Law at Boston University Schools of Medicine and Public Health, commented several years later that the Baby Doe rules and investigative squads were "counterproductive overkill. Instead of concentrating on real problems of prematurity, maternal and infant health care, and nutrition, the [Reagan] administration acted in a police-like fashion, describing physicians as child abusers and parents as accessories before the fact. This politically expedient characterization was a lie: what was really going on in America was overtreatment, not undertreatment."[2]

After hearings with medical groups and advocates for the handicapped, Congress passed legislation in 1984 that allowed exemptions for treating severely damaged infants. Doctors no longer were required to treat an infant in an irreversible coma or to provide treatment that would prolong dying and would be futile and inhumane.[3]

Nevertheless, medical groups did not believe the exemptions went far enough, because the Baby Doe Guidelines were still technically in effect and could authorize federal intervention. So the groups took their case to the U.S. Supreme Court. In 1986, the Court struck down the federal guidelines but allowed states, through their child welfare departments, to maintain the power to act as watchdogs over so-called Baby Doe cases.

Baby Jane Doe. Because of the Baby Doe regulations, a New York couple whose baby was born in 1983 had to go to court to defend their decision not to allow surgery for their infant daughter. Called Baby Jane Doe in legal documents, the infant was born with spina bifida, a genetic disorder that usually results in an opening in the spine. There was also damage to the kidneys and excess fluid on the brain. Doctors insisted on surgery to prevent even worse handicaps. They predicted Baby Jane would be bedridden for the rest of her life, perhaps in a vegetative state.

But the infant's parents refused to allow any surgery, and the baby (named Keri-Lynn) survived without extraordinary medical intervention. When Keri-Lynn was four months old, her parents allowed doctors to drain her brain. Within six months, her spine closed on its own.

Keri-Lynn has progressed far beyond her predicted fate. She is confined to a wheelchair, but she is able to attend a school for the handicapped. Intelligence tests show she "is between low-normal and educable mentally retarded," according to a report in *The Washington Post*.[4]

Many handicapped people and right-to-life advocates cite the Baby Jane Doe case as evidence that severely disabled infants should receive aggressive care. Some believe that the government should have intervened to require immediate surgery, which might have lessened Keri-Lynn's disabilities.

At the time Keri-Lynn's case was being widely discussed, bioethicist Arthur Caplan of Minnesota argued for the parents' right to make decisions regarding their daughter's treatment. In Caplan's view, government intervention was not and still is not necessary. Since the passage of the 1984 Baby Doe law, "state child welfare departments have found no cases in which hospitals or parents have been guilty of abuse or neglect" of severely disabled infants, Caplan wrote in a 1991 newspaper column. He went on:

> *In retrospect, there can be no denying that the level of misery predicted for Keri-Lynn was way off the mark. And the battle over her care did much to change attitudes among doctors, nurses and the public about the prognosis faced by kids with spina bifida and other congenital birth defects.*
>
> *But I still believe that the federal government was wrong to interfere. Her parents, while choosing a conservative course, never abandoned her and certainly never neglected her. . . . Keri-Lynn is a reminder that medicine is an uncertain science. But the battle over her medical care is also a reminder that, in the face of uncertainty, parents are in the best position to make hard choices among medical treatments of uncertain efficacy.*[5]

Other Interests at Stake. Some parents who have had to make hard choices regarding extraordinary care for their severely impaired infants say that people who have not been in their shoes should not be the ones making the decisions about their children. These strangers will not have to pay the costs, whether in financial terms or in emotional and physical strains.

In some cases, pregnant women who have learned before childbirth that their babies have severe defects have opted for abortion rather than take a chance on giving birth and letting physicians and the courts take over. To these pregnant women, aggressive action on the part of physicians to keep profoundly impaired babies alive is maltreat-

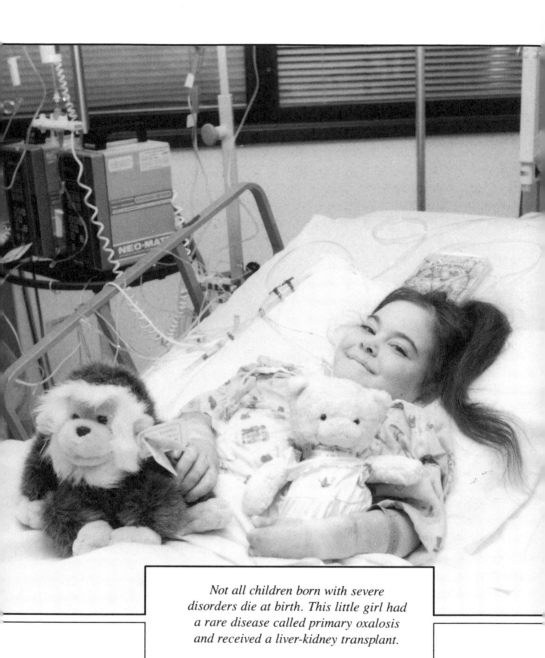

Not all children born with severe disorders die at birth. This little girl had a rare disease called primary oxalosis and received a liver-kidney transplant.

ment. In the opinion of columnist and author Jeff Lyon, "It is a great mischief for physicians, who will not have to live with the long-range effects of their actions, to present a handicapped child to parents who don't want it."

In his book *Playing God in the Nursery*, Lyon described dozens of instances when parents faced the painful issue of whether death was the most merciful choice for a profoundly disabled infant. The results of saving a child were worse than death in some cases, according to Lyon. Consider what happened to the West family of California.

Brian, the child of John and Susan West, was born in 1980 with Down syndrome and an abnormal esophagus. The Wests would not consent to surgery to correct the esophagus, because the success rate for the operation was poor, and because Brian would have to be subjected to repeated medical procedures over the years to keep the esophagus open. The Wests believed it would be more humane to allow Brian to die.

Hospital officials would not accept the Wests' decision and obtained a court order allowing surgeons to operate. Then the state welfare department charged the Wests with child neglect. A lawyer advised the Wests not to contest the charges, and Brian became a ward of the court. It was a humiliating experience for the Wests, who were being treated like criminals even though they were sure they had made a loving and merciful decision for their child.

Doctors kept Brian alive for a little over two years. But his short life was little more than pure torture, with numerous visits to the hospital and multiple surgeries. Doctors waited several weeks before attempting the first operation, and during that time Brian was fed liquids through his abdomen. He endured several sieges of pneumonia, and once his heart stopped, but medical personnel revived him.

After Brian underwent experimental surgery to reconstruct his esophagus, stomach acid backed up, causing extremely painful burns on his skin. The Wests reported that when they visited their son, they found him screaming in agony. For weeks, his hands and feet were tied down so that he would not aggravate his surgical wounds.

When the wounds healed, they formed scar tissue, and the surgeon repeatedly had to dilate (open) the esophagus, which never did function. Through all of this, there were numerous infections. In November 1982, Brian suffered breathing problems and was put on a respirator in the hospital. When the respirator was removed, doctors found that Brian was blind and brain-damaged. After five weeks in intensive care, he died.[6]

Brian's parents, along with others whose seriously impaired infants have survived for a few months or years through intensive use of medical intervention, do not believe that these extraordinary measures can be justified. They believe they were forced into situations over which they had no control.

Some parents who have cared for extremely impaired children for many years feel their lives have been destroyed. There is little relief, because most families do not get needed breaks from daily caregiving and do not receive the necessary financial and emotional support. Some studies show that endless strain leads to a high rate of divorce among couples with handicapped children.

In addition, siblings may suffer emotional and behavior problems because their parents must spend so much time with a disabled child. Able youngsters also are expected to act in mature ways and, sometimes, to take on responsibilities unsuited to their developmental years.[7] However, some of these problems could be lessened if there were a national commitment to help families with severely disabled children.

Yet some parents of disabled youngsters say their lives have been changed positively because of their children. They do not regret any sacrifices they have made and take great pride in their children's growth and accomplishments. Certainly many disabled children have become "handiable" adults—highly productive and able to contribute to society when barriers and prejudices against them have been removed.

Some parents and their disabled children become members of such organizations as The Arc and TASH (The Association for Persons with Severe Handicaps). Both groups serve people with severe mental disabilities. Along with advocates for people with physical disabilities, they have issued resolutions opposing the withdrawal of life support for severely damaged infants and for people labeled comatose or in a persistent vegetative state. Because comatose people and those in a vegetative state appear to share characteristics similar to those of people labeled profoundly mentally retarded, The Arc believes that helping to bring about their death is the ultimate denial of their civil and human rights.

Concerns of Disabled People. People with disabilities and advocates for handicapped individuals believe that courts should continue to intervene in Baby Doe cases. In late 1989, the U.S. Commission on Civil Rights released a report titled "Medical Discrimination Against Children with Disabilities," which concluded that some medical practitioners deny lifesaving treatment to severely disabled infants. In its study, based on a random survey of physicians and reports from hospital workers, the commission concluded that physicians denied treatment because of "erroneous judgments concerning the quality of life" and their belief that severely disabled babies would place heavy burdens on families and taxpayers.

After publication of the report, some physicians strongly objected, arguing that medical decisions—whether for an infant or adult—have to be based in part on the quality of life that will result. Not taking that into account is unrealistic and perhaps the same as abuse. Critics of the report also said the commission had ignored the fact that doctors fear lawsuits, so they are more apt to order treatment for fatally damaged infants, overriding the wishes of parents who do not want their impaired newborns hooked up to life-support systems.

On the other side, advocates for people with disabilities contended that many parents have come to expect nothing less than perfect children, so they are apt to deny consent for extensive life-support or intensive-care treatment for an impaired infant. At the time of the Baby Doe case, the editor of *The National Right to Life News* wrote: "The moment parents and physicians learn the baby is not going to be a track star/nuclear physicist, they begin subconsciously to think of the little one as some sort of recyclable aluminum can."[8]

Many people believe this view is an outright distortion. But it reflects a concern of some who have survived with disabilities. They believe that the widespread attitude of trying to create a child who will measure up to some standard of physical and mental perfection has helped maintain a long-standing prejudice against handicapped people.

Dianne Piastro, a disability rights activist, has dedicated her syndicated column to overcoming discrimination and prejudice against people with disabilities. In 1991 she wrote:

How many times have you heard someone say, "I'd rather be dead than disabled?" . . . When people say that, I want to believe it's out of fear of

the unknown, but it still invalidates my experi-
ence as a disabled person. . . . When removal of
life-support systems is requested by severely dis-
abled people, or their families, the courts usually
grant their wishes. When those same people,
however, need emotional and financial support to
live independently or be assisted at home, it is
usually denied.

There is something hideously wrong with
this. . . . It makes choosing death almost pre-
dictable when you're denied equal opportunities
to live; when you're devalued and often perceived
only in terms of what you cannot do.[9]

Tough Questions About Brain-Absent Newborns. In recent years, another issue concerning damaged newborns
has become part of the right-to-die and euthanasia debate.
It centers on anencephalic infants such as Baby Theresa,
born on March 21, 1992, in Fort Lauderdale, Florida. The
daughter of Laura Campo and Justin Pearson, Theresa was
born with only part of her brain—the brain stem, which
controls reflexes such as breathing and heartbeat. As with
many anencephalic infants, most of Theresa's skull just
above the eyes was missing.

No one is sure what causes anencephaly, a condition
that occurs in two out of every thousand fetuses in the
United States and six of every thousand worldwide. Most
anencephalic infants are stillborn (born dead), and only
about four hundred to five hundred a year live longer than
a few minutes after birth, according to a neonatologist (a
physician specializing in newborns) at Broward General
Medical Center in Fort Lauderdale.[10]

Anencephaly can be detected with a simple blood test
taken between the fifteenth and twentieth weeks of a
woman's pregnancy, a time period during which a woman

The parents of Baby Theresa mourn the loss of their nine-day-old baby. Before she died, the infant, born with only a brain stem, became the center of a legal controversy when her parents asked that she be declared brain-dead in order to donate her organs.

may choose to have an abortion. Although the test is inexpensive, not all women get one, because they may not be part of a high-risk group—those over age thirty-five or those who may be likely to pass on defective genes. Since Laura Campo was not in a high-risk group, she did not have the test. But when she was in the late stage of her pregnancy, her baby's condition was revealed by an ultrasound test.

After Theresa was born, doctors did not expect her to live for more than a few minutes, but she survived for several days. When Theresa's breathing began to falter, she was placed on a respirator. Her parents requested that she be declared brain-dead so that doctors could remove her vital organs. They hoped her organs would help other newborns needing transplants and would give meaning to Theresa's tragedy. If all brain functions stopped, the organs would deteriorate and could not be used.

Lawyers for Theresa's family went to the Broward County Court to gain legal permission to have Theresa declared brain-dead. But the county judge denied the petition. According to a 1988 Florida law, Theresa was alive. All brain activity had to cease before anyone could be declared dead.

Yet prior to 1988, the law considered an anencephalic infant brain-dead, according to Walter G. Campbell, Jr., attorney for Theresa's parents. He noted that decisions about when a patient was brain-dead used to be determined by doctors in consultation with family members. If a patient suffered brain damage that prevented basic functions necessary for human life, then that person could be declared dead.

The judge allowed removal of any nonvital organs, but required that the procedure be done without endangering Theresa's life. Transplant experts at the University of Miami explained that a kidney could have been removed for transplant in an adult, since an infant kidney can expand rapidly. Tissue around the kidney and an artery would have been needed also, which would have been very risky.[11]

Baby Theresa died on March 30, 1992, at nine days old. But her short life focused once more on questions: Does a person exist without higher brain functions? If a body merely breathes, does that mean the entity is a person, and is hastening death the same as killing?

In November 1992, the Florida Supreme Court upheld the lower court's ruling preventing a brain-absent baby from being declared dead so that the organs can be used for transplants.

But most doctors in organ transplant programs say anencephalic infants should be declared brain-dead because they have no potential for "recovery" and they could save other infants' lives. In fact, surgeons at the Loma Linda University Medical Center in California acted on this belief in 1987. Doctors there transplanted a heart from an anencephalic infant born in eastern Canada into a newborn from British Columbia.

Known as Baby Gabriel, the anencephalic infant met the Canadian legal criteria for brain-death. Canadian physicians were able to keep the body of Baby Gabriel as well as other anencephalic infants alive by placing them on respirators. In effect, the babies became incubators for their own organs until those organs could be removed for transplanting.

Medical personnel flew Baby Gabriel to Loma Linda for surgery. After news stories explained details of the transplant, Loma Linda became the focus of heated debates. A year later the medical center halted the program under which it accepted and used organ donations from anencephalic infants.

The debate over the use of organs from brain-absent babies has continued in the United States, as is clear from the Baby Theresa case. In the opinion of Les Olson, director of the Organ Procurement Program at the University of Miami School of Medicine, if medical professionals were given a choice, they would "always choose the lives of babies who can be helped over the life of the baby who is going to die anyway. It's a practical decision that makes medical and moral sense to most people. . . . [But] by our current law, it would be murder."[12]

Many who oppose keeping an anencephalic infant alive for the purpose of harvesting organs say the practice is grotesque or barbaric. Yet there has not been the same kind of opposition in several well-publicized cases where pregnant women were seriously injured or terminally ill and were kept alive only to serve as incubators for the fetuses they carried.

Once again, as with other euthanasia issues, there appears to be no middle ground. But in any ethical dilemma the questions have to be continually discussed because, as Anne Davis, a University of California ethicist, noted, there is no such thing as a perfect solution. Rather, the most important aspect is the process of evaluating ethical policies, which do not all "come down from Mount Sinai. They can be rewritten and changed."[13]

Legal Actions

Because public policies related to euthanasia issues are not set in stone, activists have organized to bring about change. Some have worked to reduce government and medical intervention in family decisions regarding severely impaired infants or in choices that adults make about their own dying process. Others have worked to establish more government control in such matters.

Much of the legal effort over the past few years, however, has centered on whether a person who is terminally ill can be assisted in the dying process or can hasten dying by refusing medical treatment. Attention also has focused on whether families have or should have the authority to make medical decisions for incapacitated adult members.

In the *Cruzan* decision, the U.S. Supreme Court ruled that the state of Missouri was within its rights to disregard family members' statements about Nancy's wishes and to demand "clear and convincing evidence" that she would want to discontinue life support. New York State also requires such evidence.

Some observers believe the *Cruzan* ruling gave state governments far too much power over citizens' lives and interfered with family decision-making. Although the Supreme Court decision in *Cruzan* did not change laws in other states, it set the stage for legal battles. In some states, legislators have passed laws restricting the role of individuals and family members in choices about life-and-death matters.

Family Decision-Making. Not quite half the states, either through legislation or court rulings, permit families to make health care decisions for relatives who are incompetent. Families might decide to withhold or withdraw medical treatment or to maintain whatever life support is available. For example, in Minnesota the wishes of eighty-seven-year-old Helga Wanglie as expressed by her family were upheld in an unusual case.

After surgery to repair a fractured hip in December 1989, Helga Wanglie developed pneumonia and her lungs failed. She was connected to a respirator but was unconscious, remaining that way for most of a year. During that time, her heart stopped, and although doctors revived her, she suffered severe brain damage.

In mid-1990, hospital personnel advised that the respirator be turned off because it was not in the patient's best interest. They believed they were being forced to provide inappropriate medical care. But the family refused, saying that Wanglie did not want her life "snuffed out." Hospital administrators eventually took the case to court in February 1991, but in July the court refused to allow the hospital to turn off the respirator, upholding the family's right to act on Wanglie's behalf. Wanglie died three days after the court ruling.

Prior to the decision, Susan M. Wolf, a lawyer for the Hastings Center medical ethics research institute, said the hospital was "trying to turn back the clock and reverse the whole thrust of modern biomedical ethics." She predicted that if the hospital won the case, "patients or the people they designate to speak for them [would] lose decisional authority that we have all been fighting long and hard to secure for them."[1]

Many right-to-die groups, the American Medical Association, and others agreed. They believe that as long as families act in good faith, they should be able to make decisions for incompetent family members. That was the point that Justice William J. Brennan made in his dissenting opinion in *Cruzan*. Brennan noted that he could not quarrel with the Court's view that close family members do not always abide by a patient's wishes. But such a view "leads only to another question: Is there any reason to suppose that a State is more likely to make the choice that the patient would have made than someone who knew the patient intimately? To ask this is to answer it."[2]

Living Wills. One way that individuals and families can help protect their right of choice in end-of-life matters is with a living will. A living will is a legal document stating a person's wishes about medical treatment. It is an advance directive—instructions for the type of health care individuals want if they are eventually unable to make decisions on their own.

Usually only patients who are terminally ill can be covered by a living will, although court cases have established that treatment can be withdrawn when a person is in a persistent vegetative state. At the end of 1991, forty-one states and the District of Columbia had established living will laws.

The National Right to Life Committee (NRLC) has consistently opposed living will legislation, and the organization now offers an alternative to members—a document called the "Will to Live" with the subtitle "General Presumption for Life." According to the NRLC, the legal

William J. Brennan, Jr., who served on the United States Supreme Court from 1956 to 1990, was known for his strong support of individual liberties.

A living will is used to spell out a person's wishes regarding medical treatment. All fifty states have laws recognizing living wills.

form is needed to counteract right-to-die groups that have brought about "public acceptance of assisted suicide, mercy killing, and euthanasia, replacing the [once] accepted ethic that the lives of all human beings are of equal and inestimable dignity."

In a 1992 newsletter, NRLC claimed that "many health care facilities are promoting living wills and other documents slanted toward rejection of treatment and even food and water." NRLC advised its members to complete a Will to Live form in order "to lessen the real and growing danger that you may be starved or denied necessary medical treatment when you cannot speak for yourself."[3]

NRLC's proposed will is a legal document that helps assure a person's wishes will be honored, but the NRLC statements about living will laws are misleading. Some living will forms may include statements directing physicians to withdraw life-prolonging procedures, but the forms may also require that nutrition and hydration be provided. Although a few states have passed legislation that allows withholding food and water in cases of terminally ill patients, other states have blocked such statutes. Indiana is one of them.

Two years in a row, during the 1991 and 1992 legislative sessions, Indiana lawmakers rejected bills that would have allowed withholding artificial nutrition and hydration if a patient is in a permanent vegetative state. Indiana Right to Life and Citizens Concerned for the Constitution, two groups that have lobbied consistently against abortion, claimed food and water were necessities of life that doctors were obligated to provide. They likened the bills to legalizing physician-assisted suicide.

Some states allow the use of state-specific forms prepared by the Society for the Right to Die, which merged with another organization called Concern for Dying in

1991. The combined organization is known as Choice in Dying, which describes the group's purpose: to educate Americans about their end-of-life choices and to help ensure that people do not have to accept medical treatment they do not want.

Along with or instead of living will legislation, some states have passed Durable Power of Attorney Acts or Health Care Proxy laws. These statutes permit a person to appoint someone to act on her or his behalf in regard to medical treatment. This legally appointed agent has the power to refuse or accept life-support measures for another person should that person become terminally ill and incapacitated.

State laws differ, however, as to who may be authorized to act as agent, or proxy. Judith Areen, dean and professor of law at Georgetown University Law Center, explained:

> *Typically, the statutes direct turning first to the court-appointed guardian, if there is one, then to the patient's spouse, then to the adult child (or a majority of adult children if there are more than one), then to either parent. Louisiana and Utah are careful enough to specify that to be eligible the spouse must not be judicially separated, and Texas adds that the spouse must be an adult. Six of the states authorize turning as a last resort to the patient's "nearest living relative."* [4]

Although most states allow family decision-making, surrogates may be restricted in the choices they can make for patients. States also attempt to guard against abuse by family members who serve as proxies. In some instances, laws specifically state that family members must act on behalf of the patient or be guided by a patient's intentions.

Because of the Cruzan case, the Missouri legislature in May 1991 passed legislation that allows people to designate others to make health care decisions for them if they become incompetent. The law also allows a patient's proxy to approve the removal of food and water if that was the patient's request.

Patient Self-Determination Act. Only a small percentage of Americans actually complete living wills or appoint proxies. In fact, few actually have any type of will. Some people do not make advance plans in regard to dying because they believe such matters should be left to God or Fate. Others do not think they will need a legal document, since they believe their chances of being incapacitated when near death are remote.

People may be convinced that family or friends will make the best possible decisions on their behalf, should the necessity arise. As one physician explained, "I have had a number of seriously ill patients say that their next of kin will attend to some choice if it comes up. When challenged with the possibility that the next of kin might decide in a way that was not what the patient would have chosen, the patient would kindly calm my concern with the observation that such an error would not be very important."[5]

In November 1991, a federal law called the Patient Self-Determination Act was enacted. It requires health care providers in facilities receiving federal funds to inform patients about a living will or advance directive. Critics have called the measure a "Miranda" warning for patients, like the requirement to read criminal suspects their rights after arrest. But supporters see it as a way to educate the public.

The law was designed to let patients know that they have the right to communicate their wishes about the extent of their medical treatment. No one has to complete the directive. In fact, patients may opt for another type of directive such as the "Will to Live" proposed by the National Right to Life Committee.

"Do Not Resuscitate" Orders. Another way that patients can control their medical treatment is with do-not-resuscitate (DNR), or do-not-revive, orders. It has been a long-standing practice to allow hospitalized patients who are terminally or chronically ill to sign DNRs.

Perhaps a person who has suffered from a long illness does not want to be revived if it means living in pain or hooked up to life-support systems. In such cases, patients certify that they do not want to be resuscitated if their heart or breathing stops. Hospital personnel usually are aware of and can comply with DNR orders included in a patient's file.

The situation is different, however, if a patient is at home, in a hospice, or in another facility. In an emergency, the first reaction of family members or health care professionals might be to call 911 for an ambulance and paramedics to assist a dying patient.

Paramedics are trained to resuscitate to prevent death. Suppose a patient is having a heart attack. Paramedics would immediately administer oxygen and begin some type of cardiopulmonary resuscitation (CPR)—procedures to stimulate the heart. There is little time to determine whether a patient has a DNR order or a living will stating that she or he does not want to be kept alive by artificial means. Besides, paramedics are legally bound to try to save dying patients' lives.

Because of the obvious conflict between the duties of emergency medical technicians and the wishes of some patients, nine states have passed laws that provide ways for paramedics to recognize DNR orders. In the state of

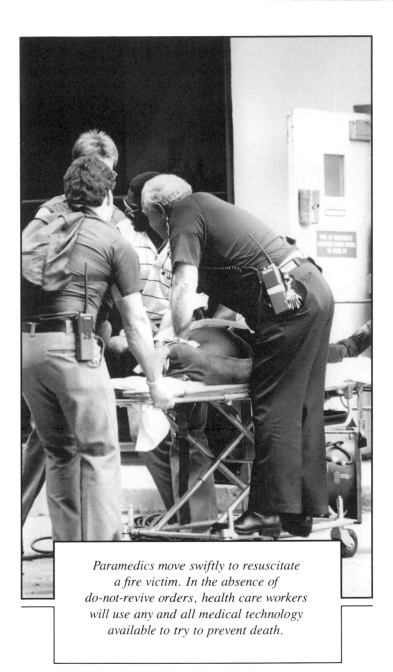

*Paramedics move swiftly to resuscitate
a fire victim. In the absence of
do-not-revive orders, health care workers
will use any and all medical technology
available to try to prevent death.*

California, for example, five counties, including the most populous, Orange County, allow patients to wear green plastic arm or leg bands that to emergency crews mean "Do Not Resuscitate."

According to a report in the *Los Angeles Times*, "Medics may administer oxygen and make other efforts to ease suffering," but they may not use CPR or other methods to revive a person. If paramedics start CPR and then discover a patient is wearing a green band, they must stop the procedure.[6]

Other states with similar DNR laws also require some kind of identification bracelet or card. And while some states limit DNR orders to patients estimated to have only six months to live, others include patients with chronic, life-threatening conditions.

Efforts to Legalize Assisted Suicide. One of the most controversial right-to-die efforts has been the campaign to legalize physician-assisted suicide. In November 1991, registered voters in Washington State had the opportunity to decide whether they would pass Initiative 119, a proposed law known as the Death with Dignity proposal. In Washington and a few other states, citizens can place a proposition on the ballot, and voters can decide whether to accept or reject it.

Initiative 119 was designed to amend the state's 1979 Natural Death Act. It expanded the definition of terminal illness to include persistent vegetative state and any condition that would result in death within six months. It also proposed that the statute should declare the specific life-support procedures that could be withdrawn on request, such as food and water, CPR, and respirators.

The final section, however, created the most discussion and debate, igniting heated reaction from around the world. It proposed that adult patients with terminal condi-

Washington State's Death with Dignity proposal (Initiative 119) failed to pass when it went to a vote in November 1991.

tions (confirmed by two doctors) be allowed to request and receive "aid-in-dying" from their physicians.

Those who backed the Death with Dignity initiative included AIDS patients, senior citizen groups, many individuals who had witnessed relatives' prolonged and painful dying, and groups such as Citizens for Death with Dignity (which sponsored the initiative), the Hemlock Society, and some liberal religious organizations. Proponents said that legalized aid-in-dying should be every citizen's basic right. They contended that people who have less than six months to live and are suffering should have the power to make private choices about their dying and have medical help to die if that is their choice.

Opponents included the Washington State Catholic Conference, which provided a major portion of the funds to defeat the initiative; other conservative religious groups; right-to-life organizations; many physicians; and hospice workers. They repeatedly argued that legalizing euthanasia would lead to great abuse. They contended that if health care professionals or others were permitted to assist people in dying, they would have too much power and would be accountable to no one. Opponents also said that if euthanasia became accepted practice, American social and legal policies would be on a slippery slope. In other words, people would be pulled toward ever more frequent use of euthanasia.

Patients, for example, might feel pressured to hasten their dying so that they would not be financial and emotional burdens on their families and society. Critics argued that the more acceptable euthanasia became, the more likely that protections for defenseless people would slide away. Handicapped people, severely disabled newborns, the dependent aged, and others might be involuntarily killed as a "merciful" act.

Opponents cited another drawback: the effect of legalized euthanasia on the poor and those with little or no insurance. Increasing medical costs might prompt poor people to consider ending their own lives or the lives of seriously ill relatives who would be a drain on financial resources.

A little over 600,000 Washington voters approved the initiative, but about 700,000 voted against the proposal, defeating it. Although the initiative failed, right-to-die issues and proposals to legalize euthanasia are still being discussed and debated. In Oregon and Florida, pro-euthanasia groups are attempting to place initiatives similar to Washington's Initiative 119 before voters. California voters, in November 1992, rejected Proposition 161, which would have legalized physician-assisted suicide in that state.

Other states have been trying to clarify laws dealing with right-to-die issues so that people who do not want to prolong their dying can stop medical life support.

Margaret Pabst Battin, professor of philosophy at the University of Utah, believes that the campaign to legalize euthanasia will be a major social movement in the United States in the years ahead. She supported the Washington initiative and has stated in the past that in some instances euthanasia is a moral action based on principles of mercy, autonomy, and justice. But she also has argued that society should focus more attention on alternatives to physician-aid-in-dying, rather than becoming polarized over right-to-die legislation.[7]

In some cases, activists seem to be searching for common ground. Both opponents and supporters of the Washington initiative, for example, worked through the legislature to reform the state's Natural Death Act, although one right-to-life lawmaker attempted to block any changes in the act by proposing forty-five amendments to the bill and stalling action for three hours. However, the revised act passed, and it clearly states that dying patients can refuse life support, including feeding tubes. Reforms also call for hospitals and doctors to honor living wills or refer patients to facilities that do.[8]

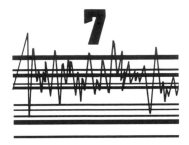

Euthanasia Concerns in Other Nations

In some cultures, such as those of China and India, it is an ancient peasant custom (still practiced in remote areas) to drown newborn girls. A female child was traditionally considered "useless" because when she grew up she would not have the means, as a boy would, to provide for her elderly parents. Therefore killing a female infant would be seen as preparation for old age; sons, not daughters, were a source of social security for the rural poor.

Of course such a practice is not part of the euthanasia debate in the United States. But it is an example of how social customs, economics, and other factors affect attitudes about euthanasia. It also calls attention to the fact that people living in poor countries or under authoritarian rule worry more about survival than about whether mercy killing is ethical or whether people have the right to die. Debates over such issues are confined primarily to affluent, industrialized nations.

Euthanasia in the Netherlands. Like Americans, the Dutch have been debating the morality of legalizing euthanasia since the 1970s. For decades, the Dutch tolerated euthanasia even though it was illegal. That is, physicians who performed euthanasia were not prosecuted if they followed strict guidelines. However, a Dutch physician could not be certain of immunity from prosecution. As a result, Dutch doctors did not always report helping terminally ill patients die.

Although no one could be sure what percentage of deaths each year were a result of euthanasia practices, anti-euthanasia forces have insisted that Dutch doctors were performing euthanasia at an alarming rate, perhaps up to 20,000 cases annually. In contrast, the Dutch Society for Voluntary Euthanasia said that doctors helped patients die in an estimated 3,000 to 5,000 cases a year.

In 1990, members of the Dutch parliament set up a commission to study not only the performance of euthanasia, but also the varied end-of-life decisions that doctors have made. The Dutch Department of Public Health and Social Medicine reported the findings in the fall of 1991. Out of 128,786 deaths recorded during 1990, an estimated 1.8 percent (about 2,300) were the result of requests for euthanasia—doctors injected lethal doses of drugs. Doctor-assisted suicide occurred in 0.3 percent (about 400) of the total deaths. Physicians provided aid-in-dying for about 1,000 patients who did not explicitly ask for assistance.

Although the study group found that most physicians refused to aid patients in dying, they also concluded:

Many patients want an assurance that their doctor will assist them to die should suffering become unbearable. We found that about two-thirds of these requests never end up as a serious and persistent request at a later stage of the disease . . . since physicians can often offer alternatives. Many physicians who had practised euthanasia mentioned that they would be most

reluctant to do so again, thus refuting the 'slip-
pery slope' argument. Only in the face of unbear-
able suffering and with no alternatives would
they be prepared to take such action. [1]

A new law, which took effect in 1993, maintains general prohibitions against euthanasia but provides legal permission for doctors to perform euthanasia for terminally ill patients who request aid in dying.[2] With this legislation, euthanasia is allowed only under certain conditions, which include the following: If a terminally ill patient requests aid in dying, the request must be voluntary. Patients must be suffering intolerable pain from which there is no relief. An attending physician must consult with another doctor to determine that the patient is near death. Doctors must report mercy killings to the proper authorities.

Many Americans have criticized the Dutch practices. Carlos F. Gomez, who conducted an extensive study of euthanasia in the Netherlands, concluded that there is great potential for abuse. He wrote:

I remain open to the possibility that the practice
of euthanasia may be controlled, though it
stretches my imagination to see precisely how
this would occur. . . . Those in the United States
who point to the Netherlands as a public policy
model for assistance with suicide have not, I
would suggest, looked carefully enough. If the
Netherlands—with its generous social services
and universal health coverage—has problems
controlling euthanasia, it takes little effort to
imagine what would happen in the United States,
with a medical system groaning under the strain
of too many demands on too few resources." [3]

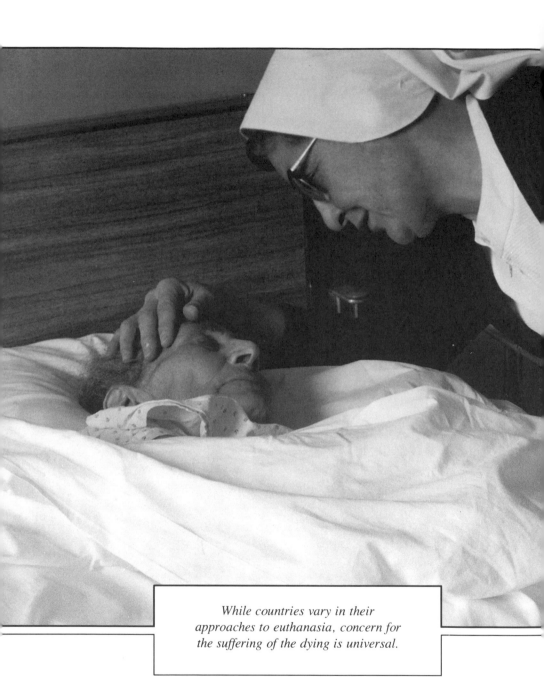

While countries vary in their approaches to euthanasia, concern for the suffering of the dying is universal.

German Views on Aid-in-Dying. Germans absolutely reject the idea of physician-aid-in-dying and believe the Dutch are out on the proverbial slippery slope, according to Margaret Battin, philosophy professor at the University of Utah. Apparently, "Germany still does not trust its physicians, remembering the example of Nazi experimentation," Battin noted in a medical journal paper comparing euthanasia in the Netherlands, Germany, and the United States.

It is not a violation of German law, however, to help a person commit suicide if that person is intent on committing the act. A person who chooses suicide may receive support from the German Society for Humane Dying, which provides information on how to obtain and use a fatal dose of drugs.

According to Battin, the two different approaches to aid-in-dying lead to ethical problems. In Germany patients may make decisions about suicide because of a serious or terminal illness but may have little or no contact with medical professionals who might be able to offer treatment or other alternatives. Without medical supervision, people who receive aid-in-suicide may choose unreliable or inappropriate methods. And there is the risk "that the means for suicide will fall into the hands of other persons," Battin wrote.[4]

The BMA Report. Several years ago, the British Medical Association (BMA) issued a report on a survey of medical professionals that was conducted to learn how doctors view euthanasia. It showed that most believe laws prohibiting euthanasia should remain in force. Physicians made a distinction, though, between active euthanasia and nontreatment that allows a terminally ill person to die.

The BMA report concluded that it was ethical in many cases for a doctor to honor patient autonomy and to comply with a patient's request not to prolong life, offering drug treatment to relieve suffering even if the treatment hastened death. Yet patients "do not have the right to demand treatment which the doctor cannot, in conscience, provide," the BMA stated. "Patients cannot and should not be able to *require* their doctors to collaborate in their death. If a patient does make such a request there should be a presumption that the doctor will not agree."

The BMA also declared that young and severely disabled patients who request aid-in-dying should receive counselling "to reaffirm the value of the person, and to counter pressure which may be created by the feeling of being unloved and an embarrassment or inconvenience to those upon whom the patient is wholly dependent." In decisions regarding severely malformed infants, the BMA cautioned against legalizing active euthanasia but added, "there are circumstances where the doctor may judge correctly that continuing to treat an infant is cruel and that the doctor should ease the baby's dying rather than prolong it by the insensitive use of medical technology."[5]

Canadian Dilemmas. Canada also has been examining right-to-die issues and euthanasia. Most Canadians believe that people should have a choice in their dying, and 75 percent of Canadians surveyed in late 1991 said physicians ought to be able to perform mercy killing.

A dramatic case in Quebec in 1992 called attention to the question of whether a person has the right to make decisions about living or dying. Nancy B., as she was called in news reports, was paralyzed from the neck down because of a rare neurological disorder. The twenty-five-year-old had lived for two and a half years with the aid of a respirator and wanted to end what she said was "no longer a life." She wanted her respirator disconnected, and when hospital staff would not grant her request she refused to eat.

Nancy B.'s Quebec City attorney admired
her client's courage: "She made the
decision she had to make. It was
her choice. It was her life."

Eventually, she was able to have a lawyer take her case to court. A Quebec Superior Court judge ruled in Nancy B.'s favor, but not before visiting her and expressing his hope that she would change her mind. However, Nancy B. exercised her right to refuse medical treatment. Her parents and brother and two sisters were with her on that morning—February 13, 1992. She was sedated and her respirator was unplugged. Seven minutes later she died.[6]

Some people would say that Nancy B.'s decision allowed her to die with dignity and thus was a "good death." But others would contradict that conclusion. Determining what is a good death is just one more aspect of the ever-widening right-to-die debate.

What is a
Good Death?

Clearly, as in Nancy B.'s case and in others that have been presented thus far, some people find ways to manage their own dying and to achieve what they see as a "good death" or "good dying." But how does anyone determine what a good death is? To some people, death is always "bad" and is associated with negative images such as grief, loss, and sometimes terrible trauma experienced by those still living.

Perhaps one way to describe a good death is to say what it is not. For example, it is not an act of desperation and despair, as would be the case with a person who suffers from temporary depression and is suicidal. With such a disorder, a person is not likely to think clearly about other options available and may contemplate suicide as a way out of a miserable but changing or changeable situation. As suicide prevention workers have frequently pointed out, people who are suicidal usually have given up hope and feel they are useless and cannot be helped. But that is not the case. With treatment provided by health care professionals and others, depressed people can find other ways to deal with their problems.

Those who seek a good death and advocate the concept of making choices about death are referring to actions that can be taken when people are terminally ill and want to have a say in the way they will die. Of course, there is no single way to determine what those actions will or should be, because each person may have a different idea of how she or he wants to die.

Many people think of good dying as ending life quietly and peacefully after long, productive years, causing no great distress to loved ones. The dying process may be a religious experience, allowing one to transcend mortal things and pass on to another existence. Good dying might also mean ending life suddenly without pain or suffering.

"A Graceful Passage." Arnold Beisser, a physician who became paralyzed at the age of twenty-four because of polio and has long depended on others for care, calls good dying "a graceful passage." In a popular book by that title, he described several instances of people dying with dignity and grace.

One elderly woman endured a long and painful hospitalization, but because of a sincere religious belief that she was accepting "God's will," she was able to die peacefully. Another woman had been successful in business and had controlled and manipulated people most of her life, but she made great efforts to heal relationships with family members and friends before she died. Still another instance involved an elderly theologian and his wife, both of whom had become seriously ill and needed constant medical care; they were both very religious but felt there was little dignity left and together ended their lives.

Although these people died in different ways, Beisser pointed out that they all had some control over their lives and their approach to death, and this allowed them to die

Attendees at a senior center learn about advance directives. Appointing someone else to make health care decisions in the event that you are unable to communicate is an important step in self-determination.

with grace. Even in the case of the double suicide, he noted that the couple "saw no more purpose in prolonging life when they had no more to give to it." In his view they did not act in a reckless manner; instead they took a rational approach to death and dying.

Making a decision whether to live or die is an "awesome choice" that "belongs not to courts, to attorneys, to hospitals, to doctors, to nurses, or to any other group, but to the person whose life it is," Beisser wrote. "That is the essence of being alive—being able to choose; otherwise we live only by instinct, like insects, or by the orders of others, like robots. And the most important choice one ever has is between life and death."

However, Beisser repeatedly emphasized that the decision to end one's life should be a reasonable choice—not motivated by emotional reactions to what appears to be a desperate situation. He described many instances in which he was immobilized, in constant pain, and in great despair, wishing for release, but he found that these conditions changed. "The change often comes from some unexpected place when all seems lost and hopeless," he wrote. Sometimes friends and health care workers helped to bring about a more positive approach, but he also "learned to take an active part in making the change," which is what much of his writing is about.[1]

Many people who have permanent disabilities or incurable diseases find ways to cope with their pain and the fact that they may not live out a normal life span; they do not try to bring an immediate end to living. For example, facing death is a constant with the Ray family in Florida. Three of Louise and Clifford Ray's four children were infected with HIV, the virus that causes AIDS.

The three boys, Ricky, Robert, and Randy Ray, were born with hemophilia, a hereditary disease in which the blood does not clot properly. A hemophiliac must receive blood transfusions frequently, and the boys contacted HIV through contaminated blood used during their regular treatments. When their condition became known, they were subjected to harassment and discrimination because of misunderstandings about how AIDS is transmitted. But the boys and the rest of the family tried to maintain a positive attitude and a fighting spirit. They appeared on many television talk shows to help educate people about HIV and its effects.

In March 1991, Ricky, the oldest boy, learned that the virus he carried had developed into full-blown AIDS, which left no doubt that his life would be shortened. "I knew it was coming," he said. "The only thing I'm worried about is leaving my family behind. That's the only thing that scares me. I guess I'll just live it a day at a time."[2] On December 13, 1992, Ricky Ray died.

Taking it a day at a time is one more way that some people who know their death is likely to come soon try to make a "graceful passage." It is part of the process of dying with dignity.

More Than a Right to Die. Dying with dignity is one of the stated goals of advocates for right-to-die legislation— those who want laws established to allow individuals to have a say in the way they will die. To accomplish a dignified death, however, requires far more than assuring the right of self-determination.

For one thing, many observers believe there should be more realistic discussion about the fact that death and dying are part of life. In U.S. culture it is common to stress youth, vibrant good health, and "perfect" physical assets. As a result, many people seem to forget that the vast majority of us never fit an artificial standard for physical perfection. Furthermore, we all age, and everyone must face death at some time. With acceptance of these facts, people might be more willing to explore diverse views on dying, including opinions on euthanasia.

Because of well-publicized cases (from Baby Doe to Nancy Cruzan to Jack Kevorkian's clients), the American public has begun to openly debate the once taboo subject of euthanasia. The public discourse will probably continue well into the future. But if the debate centers only on "right to die" versus "right to life," little will be accomplished, because there are many related issues to address, including diverse beliefs about the purpose of life and the meaning of death.

People also need to consider the way individual actions (such as performing euthanasia) affect a total society, how we can better care for and include dependent and vulnerable members of our community, and what actions can be taken to improve our health care system. None of the issues can be resolved easily or quickly. But taking the time to consider the varied aspects of euthanasia before making it a part of national policy seems the wisest course in a matter as final as death.

In the many opinions on the right to die published and aired in recent years, there appears to be general agreement that people should be able to exercise their right of self-determination; individuals should be able to make rational decisions about their own death when terminally ill, or be able to appoint someone to make those decisions for them. But that individual choice should always be balanced with constant efforts to find cures for diseases like AIDS and cancer and to provide proper health care so that suffering and requests for euthanasia are minimized. "In short, we want to be *allowed* to depart but we want to find *reason* to stay," as one commentator explained it.[3]

In an ideal society, then, people would respect the value of all life and try to make it meaningful. Within that ideal framework, people also would have the freedom to make responsible choices (without infringing others' rights) about personal life-and-death matters.

Notes

Chapter One

1. Case discussed in James Rachels, *The End of Life* (Oxford and New York: Oxford University Press, 1985), pp. 100–105. Also: Jeff Lyon, *Playing God in the Nursery* (New York: W.W. Norton, 1985), pp. 201–203. Derek Humphry and Ann Wickett, *The Right to Die* (Eugene, Oregon: The Hemlock Society, 1990), pp. 240–242.
2. Quoted in Diane M. Gianelli, "Death on Hold," *Chicago Tribune*, September 26, 1988.
3. U.S. Supreme Court decision reprinted in Robert M. Baird and Stuart E. Rosenbaum, *Euthanasia* (New York: Prometheus Books, 1989), pp. 179–187.
4. Associated Press, "Cruzan's Dad: 'She Didn't Die in Vain'," *Chicago Tribune*, December 29, 1990. Also: Associated Press, "Nancy Cruzan Dies, But the Issue Lives On," *Chicago Tribune*, December 27, 1990. Malcolm Gladwell, "Court Rules Woman Has Right to Die," *The Washington Post*, December 15, 1990. Pamela Warrick, "The Right to Live or Die," *Los Angeles Times*, January 10, 1991.
5. Ron Hamel, ed., *Active Euthanasia, Religion, and the Public Debate* (Chicago: The Park Ridge Center, 1991), p. 36.

6. Timothy Quill, "My Patient's Suicide" (from "Death and Dignity: A Case of Individualized Decision Making," in the *New England Journal of Medicine*, March 7, 1991), *Harper's Magazine*, May 1991, pp. 32–33.
7. Quoted in Robert Steinbrook, "Support Grows for Euthanasia, *Los Angeles Times*, April 19, 1991.
8. Betsy I. Davenport, "Why Find Euthanasia Attractive?" *The Oregonian* (Portland), May 25, 1991.
9. Case discussed in Richard W. Momeyer, *Confronting Death* (Bloomington: Indiana University Press, 1988), pp. 123–146.

Chapter Two

1. Edwin R. DuBose, "A Brief Historical Perspective," in *Active Euthanasia, Religion, and the Public Debate*, pp. 17–24. Also: Derek Humphry and Ann Wickett, *The Right to Die*, pp. 1–10. Glen Evans and Norman L. Farberow, Ph.D. "Introduction: The History of Suicide," in *The Encyclopedia of Suicide* (New York and Oxford: Facts on File, 1988), pp. vii–xxvii.
2. Derek Humphry and Ann Wickett, *The Right to Die*, pp. 10–19.
3. Quoted in Russell Chandler, "Religion Confronts Euthanasia," *Los Angeles Times*, November 2, 1991.
4. Ron Hammel and Edwin R. DuBose, "Views of the Major Faith Traditions," *Active Euthanasia, Religion, and the Public Debate*, pp. 45–77.
5. Quoted in Russell Chandler, "Religion Confronts Euthanasia," *Los Angeles Times*, November 2, 1991.
6. Joan Beck, "Doctors' Dilemma: How Much Care Is Too Much Care?" *Chicago Tribune*, January 7, 1991.
7. Harry A. Cole with Martha M. Jablow, *One in a Million* (Boston and London: Little, Brown & Company, 1990), p. 236.
8. Council on Scientific Affairs and Council on Ethical and Judicial Affairs, "Persistent Vegetative State and the Decision to Withdraw or Withhold Life Support," *Journal of the American Medical Association* (January 19, 1990), p. 429.

9. Sidney H. Wanzer, et al., "The Physician's Responsibility Toward Hopelessly Ill Patients: A Second Look," the *New England Journal of Medicine* (March 30, 1989), pp. 844–849.
10. Quoted in James D. Davis, "Killing Yourself," *Sun Sentinel* (Fort Lauderdale), January 16, 1992.
11. Jason Robb, "The True Criminal," Voice of the People, *Chicago Tribune*, May 18, 1989.

Chapter Three

1. Richard A. Knox, "Poll: Americans Favor Mercy Killing," *Boston Globe*, November 3, 1991.
2. Quoted in Greg W. Taylor with Derek Wolff, Nancy Wood, and Glen Allen, "AIDS 'Mercy Killings,' " *Maclean's* (July 16, 1990), p. 14.
3. Richard Selzer, "A Question of Mercy," *The New York Times Magazine* (September 22, 1991), pp. 32–38.
4. Stevan Rosenlind, "Man Sentenced in Wife's Mercy Killing," *The Oregonian* (Portland), August 4, 1991.
5. Fred Bayles, "Debate Over the Right to Die Grows," *The Oregonian*, October 25, 1991.
6. Eric Harrison, "Man Acquitted of Abetting Ill Wife's Suicide," *Los Angeles Times*, May 11, 1991.
7. Associated Press, "Woman Commits Suicide: Dr. Kevorkian at Her Side," *Chicago Tribune*, May 16, 1992.
8. Arthur Caplan, " 'Suicide Doctor' Should Be Prosecuted, Not Praised," *Pittsburgh Press*, June 18, 1990.
9. Wylie Gerdes, "Kevorkian Has Wide Support," *Detroit Free Press*, February 8, 1992.
10. Quoted in Ellen Whitford, "Right-To-Die Debate Goes to Polls in Washington," *Atlanta Constitution*, November 2, 1991.
11. Karl M. Funkhouser, "We Should All Thank Dr. Jack Kevorkian for His Work," *Washington Times*, February 15, 1992.
12. Associated Press, " 'Dr. Death' Likens U.S. Medical Ethics to Those of Nazi Doctors," *Los Angeles Times*, November 2, 1991.
13. Jack Kevorkian, *Prescription: Medicine* (Buffalo, New York: Prometheus Books, 1991), p. 188.

14. Michael Betzold, "His Backers and Opponents Say Issue Calls for Specifics," *Detroit Free Press*, February 6, 1992.
15. Leon R. Kass, "Suicide Made Easy," *Commentary* (December 1991), pp. 19–24.

Chapter Four

1. Kathleen M. Foley, M.D., "The Relationship of Pain and Symptom Management to Patient Requests for Physician-Assisted Suicide,"*Journal of Pain and Symptom Management* (July 1991), pp. 289–297.
2. Speech delivered January 3, 1992 in Portland, Oregon.
3. Philip Yancey, "Angel to the Dying," *Christianity Today* (December 17, 1990), pp. 22–24.
4. Part of a National Hospice Organization resolution adopted in 1990.
5. Vicki Brower, "The Right Way to Die," *Health* (June 1991), pp. 39–43.
6. Comment after speech by Susan Tolle delivered January 3, 1992 in Portland, Oregon.
7. Speech delivered January 3, 1992 in Portland, Oregon.
8. Gayle Shirley, "Nurses Pay Price for Easing Pain of Terminally Ill," *Chicago Tribune*, July 28, 1991. Also: Barry Siegel, "Reaching Out for the Dying," *Los Angeles Times*, June 23, 1991.

Chapter Five

1. Elisabeth Rosenthal (New York Times News Service), "Premature Babies: How Best to Care," *The Oregonian*, October 6, 1991.
2. George J. Annas, "The Long Dying of Nancy Cruzan," *Law, Medicine & Health Care* (Spring/Summer 1991), p. 56.
3. Helga Kuhse and Peter Singer. *Should the Baby Live?* (Oxford and New York: Oxford University Press, 1985), pp. 11–47.
4. Sarah Glazer, "Born Too Soon, Too Small, Too Sick," *The Washington Post*, April 2, 1991.
5. Arthur Caplan, "Parents Should Decide on Care for Impaired Children," *Detroit Free Press*, February 19, 1991.

6. Jeff Lyon, *Playing God in the Nursery* (New York: W. W. Norton, 1985), pp. 174–178. Also: Jay Mathews, "Brian West's Short, Tragic Life Is Ended," *The Washington Post*, December 23, 1982.

7. Helga Kuhse and Peter Singer, *Should the Baby Live?* (Oxford and New York: Oxford University Press, 1985), pp. 140–171.

8. David Andrusko, "Death of Infant Doe: Four Years Later," *National Right to Life News*, March 27, 1986, p. 1.

9. Dianne B. Piastro, "Living With a Disability," *St. Louis Post Dispatch*, November 16, 1991.

10. Michael E. Young, Sandra Jacobs, and Melinda Donnelly, "Baby's Life Stirs Debate Over Ethics, *Sun Sentinel* (Fort Lauderdale), March 29, 1992.

11. Jim Haner, "Appeals Court Backs Ruling That Prohibits Taking Baby's Organs," *Miami Herald*, March 28, 1992.

12. Quoted in Ronnie Green, "Attempts to Donate Baby's Organs Frustrated," *Miami Herald*, March 27, 1992.

13. Speech at an "Ethical Dilemmas in Nursing" workshop at Goshen College, Goshen, Indiana, March 30, 1991.

Chapter Six

1. Quoted in Robert Steinbrook, "Hospital or Family: Who Decides the Right to Die," *Los Angeles Times*, February 17, 1991.

2. *Cruzan* v. *Director, Missouri Department of Health* opinion reprinted in Robert M. Baird and Stuart E. Rosenbaum, *Euthanasia* (New York: Prometheus Books, 1989), p. 204. Also: Judith Areen, *Law, Medicine & Health Care* (Spring/Summer 1991), p. 98.

3. "Why the Need for a 'Will to Live'?" *National Right to Life News*, March 24, 1992, pp. 10–14.

4. Judith Areen, "Advance Directives Under State Law and Judicial Decisions," *Law, Medicine & Health Care* (Spring/Summer 1991), p. 98.

5. Joanne Lynn, "Why I Don't Have a Living Will," *Law, Medicine & Health Care* (Spring/Summer 1991), p. 103.

6. Lanie Jones, "O.C.'s Terminally Ill Can Soon Halt Medics' Heroics," *Los Angeles Times*, July 14, 1991.

7. Margaret Pabst Battin, "Euthanasia is Ethical," *Euthanasia.* Opposing Viewpoints Series (San Diego, Calif.: Greenhaven Press, 1989), pp. 17–23. Also: Janny Scott, "Suicide Aid Focus Turns to California," *Los Angeles Times*, November 7, 1991.
8. Annie Capestany, "Bill Tie-Up Angers Legislators," *Seattle Times*, March 15, 1992.

Chapter Seven

1. Paul J. van der Maas, Johannes J. M. van Delden, Loes Pijnenborg, and Caspar W.N. Looman, "Euthanasia and Other Medical Decisions Concerning the End of Life," *The Lancet*, September 14, 1991, p. 673.
2. Reuters News Service, "Netherlands Considers Euthanasia Proposal," *Orlando Sentinel*, April 14, 1992.
3. Carlos F. Gomez, M.D., *Regulating Death: Euthanasia and the Case of the Netherlands* (New York and Oxford: The Free Press, 1991), p. 138.
4. Margaret P. Battin, "Ethuanasia: The Way We Do It, The Way They Do It," *Journal of Pain and Symptom Management*, July 1991, pp. 298–305.
5. "Conclusions of a British Medical Association Review of Guidelines on Euthanasia," reprinted in Robert M. Baird and Stuart E. Rosenbaum, *Euthanasia* (New York: Prometheus Books, 1989), pp. 155–158.
6. "To Live or Die," *Maclean's*, February 24, 1992, pp. 46–51.

Chapter Eight

1. Arnold R. Beisser, *A Graceful Passage: Notes on the Freedom to Live or Die* (New York: Doubleday, 1990), pp. 171, 197–204.
2. John Donnelly, "Rays Shy Away from Publicity," *Miami Herald*, December 23, 1991. Also: Associated Press, "2nd Ray Brother with AIDS Fears Future," *Orlando Sentinel*, March 19, 1991.
3. K. Danner Clouser, "The Challenge for Future Debate on Euthanasia," *Journal of Pain and Symptom Management*, July 1991, p. 311. Emphasis added.

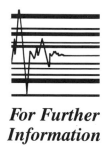

For Further Information

Recommended Reading

Books

Annas, George J. *Judging Medicine*. Clifton, N.J.: Humana Press, 1988.

Baird, Robert M. and Stuart E. Rosenbaum. *Euthanasia*. Buffalo, N.Y.: Prometheus Books, 1989.

Barnard, Christiaan. *Good Life Good Death*. Englewood Cliffs, N.J.: Prentice-Hall, 1980.

Beisser, Arnold R. *A Graceful Passage: Notes on the Freedom to Live or Die*. New York and London: Doubleday, 1990.

Bernards, Neal, ed. *Euthanasia*. San Diego, Calif.: Greenhaven Press, 1989.

Choice in Dying, David Shirley, and T. Patrick Hill. *A Good Death: Taking More Control at the End of Your Life*. Reading, Mass.: Addison-Wesley, 1992.

Cole, Harry A. with Martha M. Jablow. *One in a Million*. Boston and London: Little, Brown and Co., 1990.

Colen, B.D. *The Essential Guide to a Living Will*. N.Y., London, and Tokyo: Prentice Hall Press, 1991.

Evans, Glen and Norman L. Farberow. *The Encyclopedia of Suicide*. New York and Oxford: Facts on File, 1988.

Gomez, Carlos F., M.D. *Regulating Death: Euthanasia and the Case of the Netherlands*. New York and Toronto: The Free Press, 1991.

Humphry, Derek. *Final Exit*. Eugene, Ore.: The Hemlock Society, 1991.

————. *Let Me Die Before I Wake*. Eugene, Ore.: The Hemlock Society, 1991.

Humphry, Derek and Ann Wickett. *The Right to Die*. Eugene, Ore.: The Hemlock Society, 1990.

Hyde, Margaret O. and Lawrence E. Hyde. *Meeting Death*. New York: Walker and Company, 1989.

Kevorkian, Dr. Jack. *Prescription: Medicide*. Buffalo, N.Y.: Prometheus Books, 1991.

Kubler-Ross, Elisabeth. *On Death and Dying*. New York: Macmillan Publishing, 1969.

Kuhse, Helga and Peter Singer. *Should the Baby Live?* Oxford and New York: Oxford University Press, 1985.

Lynn, Joanne, M.D., ed. *By No Extraordinary Means*. Indianapolis: Indiana University Press, 1986.

Lyon, Jeff. *Playing God in the Nursery*. New York and London: W.W. Norton, 1985.

Momeyer, Richard W. *Confronting Death*. Bloomington: Indiana University Press, 1988.

Ogg, Elizabeth. *Facing Death and Loss*. Lancaster, Pa.: Technomic Publishing Company, 1985.

Rachels, James. *The End of Life: Euthanasia and Morality*. Oxford and New York: Oxford University Press, 1986.

Rohr, Janelle, ed. *Death and Dying*. San Diego, Calif.: Greenhaven Press, 1987.

Rollin, Betty. *Last Wish*. New York: Simon & Schuster, 1985.

Shelp, Earle E. *Born to Die?* New York: The Free Press, 1986.

Sloan, Irving J., ed. *The Right to Die: Legal and Ethical Problems*. London and New York: Oceana Publications, 1988.

Stoddard, Sandol. *The Hospice Movement*. New York: Vintage Books, 1992.

Weir, Robert F. *Ethical Issues in Death and Dying*. New York: Columbia University Press, 1986.

Weiss, Ann E. *Bioethics Dilemmas in Modern Medicine*. Hillside, N.J.: Enslow Publishers, 1985.

Wennberg, Robert N. *Terminal Choices: Euthanasia, Suicide, and the Right to Die*. Grand Rapids, Mich.: William B. Eerdmans Publishing, 1989.

Winslade, William J. and Judith Wilson Ross. *Choosing Life or Death*. New York: The Free Press, 1986.

Worden, J. William and William Proctor. *PDA* (*Personal Death Awareness)*. Englewood Cliffs, N.J.: Prentice-Hall, Inc., 1975.

Periodicals

Ames, Katrine with Larry Willson, Ray Sawhill, Daniel Glick, and Patricia King. "Last Rights." *Newsweek*, August 26, 1991, pp. 40–41.

Attoun, Marti. "The Price of Pity." *Redbook*, November 1991, pp. 60–63.

Begley, Sharon with Mark Star. "Choosing Death." *Newsweek*, August 26, 1991, pp. 42–46.

Bernstein, Amy. "Mercy Mission?" *U.S. News & World Report*, March 18, 1991, p. 22.

Birenbaum, Arnold. "The Right to Die in America." *USA Today* magazine, January 1992, pp. 28–30.

Brower, Vicki. "The Right Way to Die." *Health*, June 1991, pp. 39–44.

Bruning, Fred. "The Menace of Morality Crusaders." *Maclean's*, January 21, 1991, p. 13.

Came, Barry. "The Last Goodbye." *Maclean's*, February 24, 1992, p. 50.

Case, Thomas W. "Dying Made Easy." *National Review*, November 4, 1991, pp. 25–26.

Colasanto, Diane. "The Right-to-Die Controversy." *USA Today* magazine, May 1991, pp. 62–63.

Deacon, James. "The Right to Die." *Maclean's*, December 9, 1991, p. 49.

"Euthanasia." *Commonweal*, August 9, 1991, Special Supplement.

Fennell, Tom. "To Live or Die: Doctors and Legislators Struggle with the Ethics of Euthanasia." *Maclean's*, February 24, 1992, pp. 46–49.

Fish, Sharon. "Nancy Cruzan's Father Knew Best." *Christianity Today*, February 11, 1991, p. 6.

Fumento, Michael. "The Dying Dutchman: Coming Soon to a Nursing Home Near You." *American Spectator*, October 1991, pp. 18–22.

Gibbs, Nancy. "Dr. Death Strikes Again." *Time*, November 4, 1991, p. 78.

Gorman, Christine and James Willwerth, Suzanne Wymelenberg. "A Balancing Act of Life and Death." *Time*, February 1, 1988.

Green, Michelle and Meg Grant, Susan Hauser, Dick Mathison, Barbara Wegher, Dirk Mathison. "The Last Goodbye." *People Weekly*, November 25, 1991, pp. 129–133.

Horgan, John. "Death with Dignity." *Scientific American*, March 1991, pp. 17, 20.

Jenish, D'Arcy. "The Right to Die." *Maclean's*, June 25, 1990, pp. 24, 28.

Journal of Pain and Symptom Management (Special Issue on Euthanasia). July 1991.

Kass, Leon R. "Suicide Made Easy." *Commentary*, December 1991, pp. 19–24.

Klass, Perri. "One of the Most Agonizing Decisions a Doctor Can Make." *Discover*, February 1986, p. 12.

Lavan, Spencer. "Whose Right to Die?" *The World*, January/February 1989, pp. 8–11.

Lawton, Kim A. "The Doctor as Executioner." *Christianity Today*, December 16, 1991, pp. 50–52.

Leo, John. "Cozy Little Homicides." *U.S. News & World Report*, November 11, 1991, p. 28.

Lyle, Katie Letcher. "A Gentle Way to Die." *Newsweek*, March 2, 1992, p. 14.

McGowan, Jo. "Little Girls Dying." *Commonweal*, August 9, 1991, pp. 481–482.

Neuhaus, Richard John. "All Too Human." *National Review*, December 2, 1991, p. 45.

Pellegrino, Edmund D. "Ethics." *The Journal of the American Medical Association*, June 19, 1991, pp. 3118–3119.

Quill, Timothy E. "My Patient's Suicide." *Harper's Magazine*, May 1991, pp. 32–34.

Schmidt, Stanley. "Your Rights, Whether You Want Them or Not." *Analog Science Fiction–Science Fact*, January 1991, pp. 4–10.

Selzer, Richard. "A Question of Mercy." *New York Times Magazine*, September 22, 1991, pp. 32–38.

Stesin, Nancy. "A Matter of Life and Death." *Ladies Home Journal*, April 1991, p. 58.

Tauber, Waler F. and Richard S. Kane, William C. Morgan, and James S. Goodwin. "Mercy Killing." *The Journal of the American Medical Association*, May 1991, p. 2189.

Taylor, Greg W. with Derek Wolff, Nancy Wood, and Glen Allen. "AIDS 'Mercy Killings'." *Maclean's*, July 16, 1990, p. 59.

"To Die With Dignity." *Time.* January 7, 1991, p. 59

Vogel, Shawna. "Anencephalic Babies." *Discover*, April 1988, p. 22.

Wartik, Nancy. "Tough Calls." *American Health*, March 1992, pp. 58–62.

"What Is the 'Good Death'?" *The Economist*, July 20, 1991, pp. 21–24.

Yancey, Philip. "Angel to the Dying." *Christianity Today*, December 17, 1990, pp. 22–24.

Organizations to Contact

American Civil Liberties Union (ACLU), 132 W. 43rd St., New York, NY 10036

American Medical Association (AMA), 535 N. Dearborn St., Chicago, IL 60610

Americans United for Life (AUL), 343 S. Dearborn St., Suite 1804, Chicago, IL 60604

The Arc, P.O. Box 300649, Arlington, TX 76010

Association for Retarded Citizens of the United States, P.O. Box 6109, Arlington, TX 76005

Choice in Dying, 200 Varick St., New York, NY 10014

The Hastings Center, 255 Elm Rd., Briarcliff Manor, NY 10510

Hemlock Society, P.O. Box 11830, Eugene, OR 97440-3900

Human Life International, 7845-E Airpack Rd., Gaithersburg, MD 20879

International Anti-Euthanasia Task Force, The Human Life Center, University of Steubenville, Steubenville, OH 43952

National Hospice Organization, 1901 N. Moore St., Suite 901, Arlington, VA 22209

National Right to Life Committee, 419 7th St. NW, Suite 500, Washington, DC 20004-2293

The Park Ridge Center for the Study of Health, Faith, and Ethics, 676 N. St. Clair, Suite 450, Chicago, IL 60611

TASH: the Association for Persons with Severe Handicaps, 11201 Greenwood Ave. N., Seattle, WA 98133

Index